EXPLORING

CAREERS

Careers in Health Care

Barbara Sheen

ReferencePoint
Press®

San Diego, CA

© 2015 ReferencePoint Press, Inc.
Printed in the United States

For more information, contact:
ReferencePoint Press, Inc.
PO Box 27779
San Diego, CA 92198
www.ReferencePointPress.com

Picture Credits:
Maury Aaseng: 6
ThinkStock Images: 11, 37, 66

LIBRARY OF CONGRESS CATALOGING-IN-PUBLICATION DATA

Sheen, Barbara.
  Careers in health care / by Barbara Sheen.
     pages cm. -- (Exploring careers)
  Includes bibliographical references and index.
  ISBN-13: 978-1-60152-648-9 (hardback)
  ISBN-10: 1-60152-648-2 (hardback)
   1. Medical personnel--Vocational guidance--Juvenile literature. 2. Allied health personnel--Vocational guidance--Juvenile literature. I. Title.
  R690.S47 2015
  610.7306'9--dc23
                                                                    2013041611

Contents

In-Demand Careers

Careers in health care are among the hottest, most in-demand occupations in the United States today, and the demand is expected to grow. With an aging population, longer life expectancies, new medical treatments and technology, and the implementation of the Affordable Care Act (also known as Obamacare), which will provide more Americans with health insurance, more and more people are expected to seek health care. All of the above will have the effect of increasing the need for health care professionals. The Bureau of Labor Statistics (BLS) reports that from 2010 to 2020, total employment in the United States is estimated to increase by 14 percent. In comparison, employment in health care professions is estimated to increase by 33 percent, resulting in about 5.7 million new jobs. Similarly, the US Department of Labor (USDL) projects that from 2009 to 2020, half of the thirty fastest-growing jobs in the United States will be in health care. These occupations include home health aide, biomedical engineer, physical therapist assistant, medical sonographer, occupational therapy assistant, physical therapist aide, medical secretary, physical therapist, dental hygienist, audiologist, health educator, medical scientist, and mental health counselor. The outlook for employment in most other health care occupations is also projected to be above average. In fact, the USDL predicts that between 2008 and 2018 no other industry will add more jobs than the health care industry.

Occupations That Suit Many Personalities

Careers in health care focus on the care and treatment of sick or injured people as well as preventive care that promotes wellness. Individuals who want to help others and make a difference in the world are often drawn to a career in health care. As Bree Abbas, a blogger, health care professional, and director of student relations for MK Education, an educational organization that provides specialized training at technical schools or community colleges for health care careers, blogs: "Some people choose the healthcare field for the money, some like the flexible hours, and others just enjoy helping people. I, however, chose healthcare to make a difference in the world. There is no other career field that allows one to make such an impact on people's lives. . . . There is never a dull moment when you are helping people live. . . . Healthcare has allowed me to make my mark!"

Health care careers also attract individuals who like working with people. Medical care often involves a team effort as well as interacting with patients and their families, medical care often involves a team effort. This makes health care occupations a good fit for people who like being part of a group. Individuals who like excitement are also drawn to the health care industry. There is rarely a dull moment for professionals such as nurses, physicians, and emergency medical technicians (EMTs). Most health care occupations are far from routine. Health care professionals perform a variety of duties and often have to make quick decisions. No two days are the same in the health care industry. And since many health care occupations require professionals to be on their feet a lot, health care careers often appeal to active, energetic people.

A Versatile Field

Health care is an extremely versatile field of employment. Individuals interested in a career in health care have more than two hundred different career options to choose from. Many health care professionals work directly with ill patients in clinical care. Nurses, nurse's aides, physicians, physician assistants, physical therapists, EMTs, speech therapists, audiologists, art therapists, dentists, chiropractors, massage therapists, and psychologists are just a few of the many career paths in clinical care. Clinical care professionals work in a variety of settings. These include hospitals, private offices, clinics, specialized diagnostic or treatment facilities, nursing homes, assisted living facilities, hospices, and private homes.

Other important health care occupations suit individuals who might not be interested in providing direct care to patients. Some of these professionals help keep hospitals and medical practices running

Health Care Job Outlook

Jobs with Highest Projected Growth (by percentage), 2010–2020

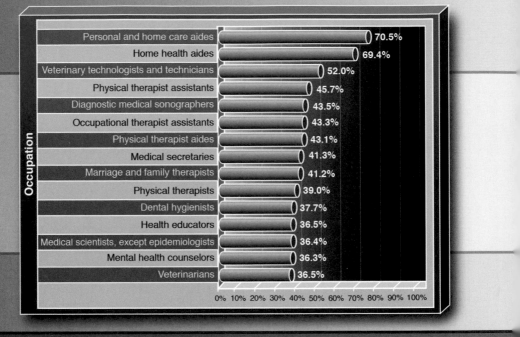

Occupation	
Personal and home care aides	70.5%
Home health aides	69.4%
Veterinary technologists and technicians	52.0%
Physical therapist assistants	45.7%
Diagnostic medical sonographers	43.5%
Occupational therapist assistants	43.3%
Physical therapist aides	43.1%
Medical secretaries	41.3%
Marriage and family therapists	41.2%
Physical therapists	39.0%
Dental hygienists	37.7%
Health educators	36.5%
Medical scientists, except epidemiologists	36.4%
Mental health counselors	36.3%
Veterinarians	36.5%

0% 10% 20% 30% 40% 50% 60% 70% 80% 90% 100%

Jobs with Highest Projected Growth (in thousands), 2010–2020

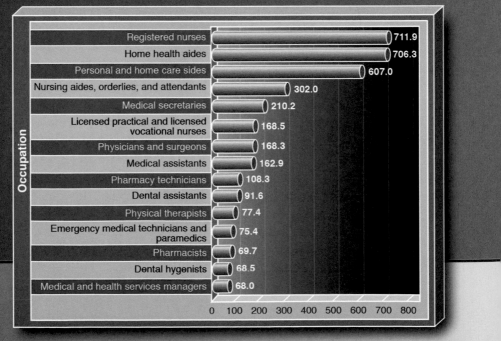

Occupation	
Registered nurses	711.9
Home health aides	706.3
Personal and home care sides	607.0
Nursing aides, orderlies, and attendants	302.0
Medical secretaries	210.2
Licensed practical and licensed vocational nurses	168.5
Physicians and surgeons	168.3
Medical assistants	162.9
Pharmacy technicians	108.3
Dental assistants	91.6
Physical therapists	77.4
Emergency medical technicians and paramedics	75.4
Pharmacists	69.7
Dental hygienists	68.5
Medical and health services managers	68.0

0 100 200 300 400 500 600 700 800

Source: The Center for Health Workforce Studies, "Health Care Employment Projections," March 2012.
http://chws.albany.edu.

smoothly. Among these professionals are health care managers and administrators, health information management technicians, medical coding and billing specialists, medical equipment preparers, and office managers.

Other nonclinical medical professionals such as medical scientists and biomedical engineers work behind the scenes in laboratories and pharmaceutical and biotech companies developing new treatments and medical equipment. Some professionals work in laboratories using microscopes and high-tech equipment to uncover information about patients' health. Cytotechnologists examine cell samples looking for abnormalities that are signs of cancer and other diseases. Medical technologists and medical lab technicians test blood samples to diagnose illnesses like HIV/AIDS. Some nonclinical medical professionals solve medical mysteries. For instance, epidemiologists seek to understand and contain disease outbreaks that threaten whole communities. Forensic pathologists determine the cause of unusual or suspicious deaths, often working with police departments. With so many different health care careers to select from, there are occupations that suit people with all types of skills, interests, and personalities.

Rewarding Careers

Health care careers are rewarding both financially and personally. In general, salaries are above average. Annual salaries for highly skilled and trained professionals such as physicians, dentists, biomedical engineers, health care administrators, medical scientists, and pharmacists can reach well into six figures. And there is lots of room for advancement. Moreover, since the health care industry is not as affected by economic downturns as other industries, health care careers offer good job security and stable employment opportunities.

The work hours, too, have a lot to offer. Some health care professionals work eight hours per day, five days per week. Others work part-time. Many work twelve-hour shifts, rotating two days on and two days off, among other flexible schedules. Working shifts gives these individuals time to balance work, family, school, and personal responsibilities.

But the rewards go beyond flexible hours and good wages. The work can be quite gratifying. As Joan Rissmiller, a health care administrator in Allentown, Pennsylvania, told the editors of *Hot Health Care Careers*, "When your act of kindness and concern puts a smile on the face of a patient who is battling a terminal disease, suddenly your paycheck is immaterial. . . . What an adrenaline rush when you realize that you play a part in the health care needs of so many individuals and that your presence has a tremendous effect on so many lives."

Emergency Medical Technician

When individuals dial 911 because they are in medical distress, an emergency medical technician (EMT) is the first medical professional at the scene. Upon receiving a 911 call involving a medical issue, an emergency dispatcher radios the EMTs, who usually work in pairs or groups, and directs them to the site of the emergency. Upon their arrival they assess the situation, check the patient's vital signs, and evaluate the patient. Then they administer immediate lifesaving treatment. If further treatment is needed the EMTs transfer the patient to an ambulance or helicopter and speed to the nearest hospital. While in transit they communicate with medical professionals at the hospital about the patient's status, and they monitor the patient and administer further treatment as needed. At the hospital the EMTs transfer the

At a Glance:

Emergency Medical Technician (EMT)

Minimum Educational Requirements
High school diploma

Personal Qualities
Calm under pressure
Physically fit

Certification and Licensing
State license

Working Conditions
Indoors and outdoors

Salary Range
About $20,917 to $49,896

Number of Jobs
As of 2013 about 226,500

Future Job Outlook
Better than average

patient to the emergency room, where they update the staff on the patient's condition and the treatment they administered.

Although not every call an EMT answers is a matter of life or death, many are. In any given day EMTs may deliver a baby, help an elderly person who has fallen, and/or care for a burn victim. The task of calming excited bystanders at the scene of a car accident often falls to the EMTs, too. The EMTs clear a path around the victims so that they can tend to them. This care often involves staunching, cleaning, and bandaging bleeding wounds, splinting fractured bones, and treating patients for shock. Treating a heart attack victim by administering CPR or providing defibrillation when a patient's heart has stopped beating is another job of an EMT. So are opening blocked airways, applying a neck brace, starting an intravenous line, and dispensing medicine. Some EMTs also drive an ambulance and prepare written reports documenting each call. And if a mass disaster occurs, EMTs are often the first on the scene. Following the 2013 Boston Marathon bombing, EMTs were on the front lines, bandaging wounds, administering oxygen and other treatments, and helping staff temporary treatment centers. In addition, EMTs are responsible for keeping their emergency vehicle in good order. Before each call EMTs check their equipment and supplies. After each call they restock their medical supplies and carefully clean their vehicle, equipment, and instruments. This prevents infectious diseases from being transmitted from patient to patient.

How Do You Become an EMT?

Education

To prepare for a career as an EMT, high school students should take classes in biology, health, psychology, and speech. If a prospective EMT plans to work in an area in which many people do not speak English, studying a foreign language, especially Spanish, is helpful. An EMT must have a high school diploma, a valid driver's license, and cardiovascular pulmonary resuscitation (CPR) certification. CPR certification training takes about three hours and is offered by the Red Cross, the American Heart Association, hospitals, fire departments, and other organizations.

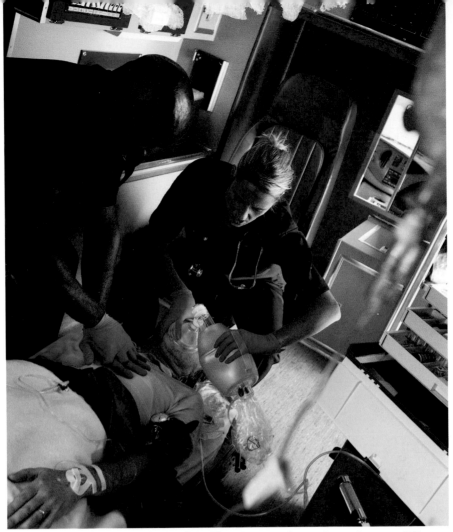

An emergency medical technician (EMT) and paramedic work together to stabilize a patient who has experienced a sudden health problem. EMTs provide immediate, life-saving treatment in many emergency situations.

EMT training requirements vary by state. The training is offered by many hospitals, police and fire departments, private EMT services, the military, technical schools, and colleges. There are three levels of EMT training: EMT basic, intermediate, and paramedic. Each level involves more training, capability, and responsibility.

EMT basic is the first level. It requires about 110 hours of training in basic emergency medical care practices. This includes hands-on instruction in dealing with medical emergencies involving fractures, soft tissues, childbirth, respiratory failure, heart attacks, bleeding, poisoning, and internal injuries. Instruction in emergency vehicle operation and maintenance is part of training. Training also includes supervised field experience. Individuals ranked EMT basic are licensed to take a patient's vital signs, administer oxygen, splint broken bones, bandage wounds, and drive an ambulance.

EMT intermediate training requires 30 to 350 hours beyond EMT basic training, depending on the state. EMT intermediate candidates learn more advanced emergency medical practices, including managing shock and administering intravenous fluids. Although the scope of practice for EMT intermediate varies by state, in general, at the EMT intermediate level individuals can do everything an EMT basic can do plus administer IV fluids and defibrillate (shock) a heart that has stopped beating.

EMT paramedic is the most advanced level of training. It requires 700 to 1,000 hours of classroom and field training beyond EMT basic training and often leads to an associate's or bachelor's degree. An EMT paramedic does all that an EMT intermediate does, plus he or she can intubate patients (use a medical device to open blocked airways), use a cardiac monitor to determine a patient's heart rhythm and treat accordingly, and dispense most medications.

Certification and Licensing

All fifty states and the District of Columbia require that EMTs be licensed. Licensing requirements vary by state. Licensing typically requires CPR certification, successful completion of EMT training, and successful completion of an exam. Some states have their own exam, while others use an exam issued by the National Registry of Emergency Medical Technicians in lieu of a state test. In addition to being used for state licensing, passing the latter exam provides an EMT candidate with voluntary national certification. Having national certification is prestigious and helps an EMT advance in his or her career.

Volunteer Work and Internships

Some volunteer rescue services, fire departments, and ambulance services let aspiring EMTs ride along on emergency calls. Doing so gives individuals the opportunity to see what the job entails. If the work seems suitable, prospective EMTs can join a volunteer rescue organization. Rescue organizations usually help volunteers get EMT basic training. Volunteering also assists an EMT when it comes to finding salaried employment. According to Scott Matin, an EMT paramedic and a member of the National Association of Emergency Medical Technicians board of directors, "The advantage is they have experience, which makes them much, much more marketable."

Skills and Personality

Being an EMT is both physically and emotionally stressful. EMTs have to be physically fit. They must be able to lift patients, carry heavy equipment on all types of terrain, including up and down stairs, and repeatedly bend and kneel. They need to be emotionally strong and resilient, too. EMTs face heartbreaking and traumatic situations on a daily basis. Even with the best of care, patients die or are hurt so badly that their lives are changed forever. Although EMTs should be compassionate and like helping people, in order to maintain their mental health and do their job well they must be able to accept these situations without becoming emotionally involved. In addition, EMTs should be calm and maintain good self-control no matter the situation. They must be able to reassure onlookers on the scene as well as panicked patients who may be emotionally unstable or under the influence of drugs or alcohol. Doing so may protect the EMT from injury at the patient's hands.

Since EMTs work in pairs or groups and work closely with responders from other agencies and emergency room staffs, being cooperative and able to work as part of a team is vital. Other important character traits include being decisive and organized. EMTs are responsible for keeping their vehicle well stocked and their equipment in working order. Having good organizational skills is necessary to do this.

Good communication skills are also essential. EMTs must quickly assess their patients. Establishing a good rapport with patients helps makes diagnosis and treatment easier. Good speaking and listening skills and an awareness of body language are key to developing this rapport. Knowledge of a second language also comes in handy. In addition to communicating with patients, EMTs must communicate with each other, with emergency dispatchers, with responders from other agencies, and with hospital personnel. They must be knowledgeable of medical terminology, be able to give a clear and concise report to hospital personnel, and be able to effectively operate and communicate over the radio. And because EMTs must prepare written reports documenting each call, they should be able to communicate in writing effectively.

Employers

EMTs work in both the public and private sectors. According to Health Guide USA, a website that provides information about careers in health care, about half of all EMTs work for private ambulance services. EMTs are also employed by fire departments, police departments, public emergency service agencies, and hospitals. Some EMTs work for more than one employer.

Working Conditions

EMTs work indoors and outdoors in all kinds of weather. Most work long hours. On average, EMTs employed by hospitals work forty-five to sixty hours per week; EMTs employed by fire departments work about fifty hours per week; and EMTs employed by private ambulance services work an average of forty-five to fifty hours per week. Some EMTs work overtime, for which they receive extra compensation. EMTs usually work odd hours. Twelve-, twenty-four-, or even forty-eight-hour shifts with three or four days off per week are common. Since medical emergencies can happen at any time, EMTs work nights, weekends, and holidays. EMTs work with partners or on teams and spend a lot of time inside an ambulance. No two workdays are exactly alike. EMTs may spend hours waiting around for a call, or they may be constantly on the go.

According to the USDL, EMTs experience more work-related injuries and illnesses than average. The physical stress of the job puts EMTs at risk of back and knee injuries as well as hearing loss from the loud siren. They also face injury from combative or mentally unbalanced patients and may be exposed to infectious diseases like hepatitis B and HIV/AIDS.

Earnings

EMTs are paid based on their EMT level, experience, education, and employer. Generally, EMT paramedics working in large metropolitan areas for a private ambulance service earn the most. The BLS reports that the average median pay for an EMT is $30,360–30,370 per year. PayScale, a website that reports salaries, says that on average,

EMTs' salaries range from $20,917 to $49,896. EMTs working full-time usually receive employee benefits such as health insurance, paid sick and vacation days, and retirement benefits.

Opportunities for Advancement

With additional training an EMT can move quickly from EMT basic to EMT intermediate to EMT paramedic. There are lots of opportunities for EMT paramedics to advance even further. EMT paramedics can get additional training for crisis situations, such as HAZMAT certification, which allows them to respond to emergency situations in which there is hazardous waste. They can also get advanced training in aeromedical safety, which prepares an EMT to work in a helicopter, or advanced training in tactical emergency medical services. With this training EMT paramedics can work with police SWAT teams using special equipment for high-risk tactical missions. In addition, EMT paramedics can advance to administrative positions supervising other EMTs, managing an ambulance service, working as an executive director of emergency services for rescue organizations, or instructing EMT candidates. Many EMT paramedics often continue their education and become registered nurses, physician's assistants, or physicians.

What Is the Future Outlook for EMTs?

As of 2013 there was a shortage of EMT paramedics in the United States. With the population aging and many volunteer rescue organizations transitioning to salaried organizations, employment opportunities for all levels of EMTs is expected to increase at a faster-than-average rate. According to the BLS, employment for EMTs is predicted to grow by 33 percent between 2010 and 2020.

Find Out More

American Ambulance Association
8201 Greensboro Dr., Suite 300
McLean, VA 22102
phone: (800) 523-4477
website: www.the-aaa.org

This organization represents and advocates for EMTs. Visitors to the website can access information about a career in emergency medical services.

Explore Health Careers.org
website: http://explorehealthcareers.org/en/Career/43/Emergency_Medical
_TechnicianParamedic

Explore Health Careers.org is a website dedicated to providing information about health care careers. The section on a career as an EMT provides an overview of the job; a video profile of an EMT; information about training, education, and wages; lists of organizations that give EMT training; and links to other resources.

National Association of Emergency Medical Technicians (NAEMT)
PO Box 1400
Clinton, MS 39060
phone: (800) 346-2368
e-mail: info@naemt.org
website: www.naemt.org

The NAEMT represents the interests of EMTs. It provides information about emergency medical careers, advocacy for emergency medical personnel, information about training and education for a career as an EMT, a list of current job openings, and a history of emergency medical services.

National Registry of Emergency Medical Technicians (NREMT)
PO Box 2933
6610 Busch Blvd.
Columbus, OH 43229
phone: (614) 888-4484
website: www.nremt.org

The NREMT provides testing for EMT certification. Prospective EMT candidates can apply for the test on its website. It also provides information about the test, about becoming an EMT, and on job postings.

Home Health Aide

What Does a Home Health Aide Do?

When people need help caring for themselves due to old age, illness, injury, or physical or mental disabilities, home health aides assist them in meeting their daily needs. In many cases this allows individuals to remain in their homes rather than to move to an assisted living facility or a nursing home. In other cases home health aides visit and provide care for individuals who make their homes in long-term care facilities. In addition, in-home hospice care—which is care for patients facing end-of-life medical conditions—almost always includes care by home health aides.

These professional caregivers perform many of the personal care duties that a spouse or relative might do for a loved one if they could be with the patient on a daily basis. Plus, under the supervision of a doctor or nurse, they often carry out simple medical procedures such as checking a patient's blood pressure, breathing, and heart rate; changing bandages and dressing wounds; emptying catheters; and administering medication.

In a typical day home health aides are likely to assist clients with bathing, dressing, grooming, and other activities involving personal hygiene. They help patients with mobility issues, which frequently involve lifting, transferring, or physically supporting patients. These professionals may prepare balanced meals for their

At a Glance:
Home Health Aide

Minimum Educational Requirements
High school diploma

Personal Qualities
Physically strong; patient

Certification and Licensing
Requirements vary

Working Conditions
In patient's homes

Salary Range
About $16,600 to $29,700

Number of Jobs
As of 2013 about 921,000

Future Job Outlook
Better than average

patients, which meet their dietary restrictions, if any. And they help with feeding when necessary. They usually assist with shopping, filling prescriptions, housecleaning, changing bed linens, and laundry. They make sure that patients take prescribed medication on schedule and assist with physical therapy exercises. They may apply hot or cold packs to patients to ease pain, or administer a massage. Taking patients to doctor appointments and reporting on the patient's progress to the family or a medical supervisor such as a nurse or social worker is also part of the job.

In addition to providing clients with physical care, home health aides provide their charges with companionship and psychological and emotional support. Since social interaction is a key component of daily living and can help keep a person's mind sharp, they often spend time chatting with their patients and listening to them talk about their lives. They also may play cards or board games with their clients, read to them, or take them on little outings such as shopping trips, visits to the barber or beauty shop, or out for lunch. These types of activities are conducive to an individual's emotional well-being. For example, a home health aide helps Bruce, a blind man whose mobility is severely limited, go on daily outings around his neighborhood. The aide pushes Bruce's wheelchair up and down the street, points out interesting sights, and stops to let him chat with neighbors. Bruce enjoys these outings. They give him a chance to stay connected with his neighbors, which is good for his emotional well-being.

Home health aides may provide private-duty services, caring for one person on a full-time basis. Or they may visit multiple patients in a day. Depending on the patient, job assignments can last just a few days or weeks, or they may last for years. Often caregivers and their clients develop a close bond. As Lisa, a Connecticut home health aide who has been working with her client, Eleanor, for more than a year explains on the National Association for Home Care and Hospice (NAHC) website: "Eleanor has Parkinson's disease and suffered a stroke three years ago. Though her mobility is somewhat limited, she is very active. We enjoy . . . shopping together, getting manicures and pedicures, and having our hair styled. Along with these activities, I assist her with all of her activities of daily living (ADLs) and physical therapy exercises. In the time that I have been with her, she has become a very special part of my life."

How Do You Become a Home Health Aide?

Education

In some cases home health aides can get a job without a high school diploma. However, most home health care agencies prefer caregivers who have a high school diploma or a general equivalency diploma. To prepare for a career as a home health aide, individuals in high school should take classes in health, family and consumer science, psychology, and speech. Studying a foreign language is also quite helpful, especially one that is commonly spoken in the area the individual wants to work. Most private home health care agencies train new personnel. Aides also gain on-the-job training. Some state programs for the elderly, adult education programs, and community colleges also offer training for aspiring aides. Training includes instruction in planning and preparing healthy meals, proper hygiene, proper fluid intake, administering medication, monitoring a patient's health, and emergency procedures.

Certification and Licensing

Certification is required for home health aides who work for agencies that receive reimbursement from the federal health care programs Medicare or Medicaid. Certification is available through the NAHC. Gaining certification involves successful completion of seventy-five hours of instruction in health care concepts and medication concerns, successful field assessment by a registered nurse, and successful completion of a written exam.

Individuals who do not work for agencies that receive money from Medicare or Medicaid are not required to have a license or certification. They can voluntarily gain certification through the NAHC. Being certified is prestigious and indicates an aide has demonstrated mastery of the profession. It helps individuals advance in their career.

Volunteer Work and Internships

Volunteering in a nursing home or assisted living facility is a good way to learn more about what home health aides do. Another way to explore a career as a caregiver is by shadowing a home health aide for at least one day. Some home health care agencies help young people arrange this. School guidance counselors and nurses may also be helpful in making job-shadowing arrangements.

Skills and Personality

Home health aides must be physically strong and fit. They often have to lift and transfer patients in and out of beds and wheelchairs and assist or support patients in rising to a standing position, walking, and ascending and descending stairs. Caregivers also need physical stamina to perform other tasks such as housecleaning, changing bed linens, walking the client's dog, or grocery shopping.

Being compassionate and emotionally strong is also vital. Some parts of the job may be unpleasant. Chores like changing soiled bed linens, emptying bedpans or catheters, and cleaning incontinent patients can be challenging. Being compassionate and emotionally strong helps home health aides cope with these tasks. And because frustrated patients who can no longer do things that they were formerly able to do may take out their frustrations on their caregiver, these same character traits help aides do their job without taking such treatment personally. It also helps them cope with patients' suffering or the death of a patient.

Patience is another important personal characteristic. Elderly clients often speak and move slowly. They may be set in their ways, demanding things be done a certain way. Caregivers need patience to do their best to accommodate their clients. Interpersonal skills are also essential. Home health aides are not just caregivers, they are companions. They should be personable and able to get along well with others. These professionals spend long periods of time with their clients. Being able to make conversation and keep their patient engaged makes their clients feel more comfortable and caregiving easier. Individuals who genuinely like people do well in this profession.

Being honest and trustworthy are also key. Home health aides have access to patients and their homes and possessions for extended periods of time, often without supervision. Patients and their families must be able to trust that the caregiver will take good care of the patient, not ignore the patient's needs or be abusive, not steal, and not take advantage of the situation.

Home health aides also need reliable transportation to get from job to job. And they should be able to cook so that they can prepare balanced meals for their clients.

On the Job

Employers

Most home health aides are employed by agencies that provide home health or hospice care. Some work for public agencies such as family services. Other caregivers are privately employed by their clients or their families. Home health aides may also be employed by continuing care retirement communities, assisted living facilities, and other residential care facilities where clients reside on a long-term basis.

Working Conditions

In general, home health aides work in their clients' homes. Those with multiple patients spend a good part of each day commuting between their patients' residences. They also drive clients to medical appointments and on outings. The hours are flexible. Most caregivers work a regular forty-hour week. Since individuals may need care twenty-four hours per day, seven days a week, aides can often choose among work schedules. There is often opportunity to work overtime for additional pay or to work part-time.

Performing tasks like transferring, lifting, and supporting patients puts home health aides at risk for back injuries or strained or pulled muscles. Despite the risk of injury, a survey conducted by the US Department of Health and Human Services of home health aides found that 72 percent of the individuals who answered the survey said that if they were choosing a career all over again, they would become a home health aide. And almost 90 percent said they were satisfied with their current jobs.

Earnings

According to the BLS, the annual mean salary for home health aides is approximately \$21,830. Salaries range from about \$16,600 to \$29,700, depending on the caregiver's qualifications and experience, the employer, and the location of employment. As of 2012 the BLS reported the following states with the highest mean wages for home health aides: North Dakota, \$29,710; Connecticut, \$28,950; Alaska, \$28,690; Vermont, \$26,890; and Rhode Island, \$26,750.

Home health aides who work full-time for home care agencies, hospice organizations, or long-term care facilities usually receive benefits that include health insurance, paid sick and vacation days, and retirement benefits. Caregivers who are employed by private individuals usually do not receive benefits.

Opportunities for Advancement

Home health aides can expect salary increases based on their experience and training. Aides who have a high school diploma, certification, and a greater level of experience are often hired to work with patients who require a higher level of medical care. These caregivers are usually paid more than aides who mainly provide personal care. Having a high school diploma, certification, and experience also helps aides to advance to supervisory positions in home health care organizations. Some home health aides start their own caregiving business. Others continue their education so that they can advance in the field of health care to positions such as licensed practical nurses or registered nurses.

What Is the Future Outlook for Home Health Aides?

The BLS reports that between 2010 and 2020, opportunities for home health aides are predicted to grow by 69 percent, much faster than the average for all other careers, including other health care careers. In fact, growth in employment for home health aides is predicted to be the largest of all health care careers. This growth is attributed to multiple factors, including an increasing elderly population. Older individuals often have health problems and require assistance with daily activities that home health aides provide. Moreover, home health care is often a less costly alternative to assisted living or other long-term care facilities. And when given a choice, many people prefer to be cared for in the comfort of their own homes.

Find Out More

Direct Care Alliance
4 W. Forty-Third St., Unit 610
New York, NY 10036
phone: (212) 730-0741
e-mail: info@directcarealliance.org
website: www.directcarealliance.org

The Direct Care Alliance is a New York organization that advocates for professional caregivers and individuals who need their services. It provides information about the profession, education, certification, and wages.

Explore Health Careers.org
website: http://explorehealthcareers.org

Explore Health Careers.org is a website dedicated to providing information about health care careers. The section on a career as a home health care aide provides an overview of the job, a link to a video about the career, and other information.

National Association for Home Care and Hospice (NAHC)
228 Seventh St. SE
Washington, DC 20003
phone: (202) 547-7424
website: www.nahc.org

The NAHC provides information about caregiving, including interviews with home health aides, publications, and news concerning the profession.

Private Duty Homecare Association
228 Seventh St. SE
Washington, DC 20003
phone: (202) 547–7424
website: www.pdhca.org

This organization is an affiliate of the NAHC. It is a trade association of private-duty caregivers. It provides information about the profession, certification, education, job postings, and links to other resources.

Mental Health Counselor

Mental health counselors help individuals with mental and emotional problems. They diagnose and treat psychological conditions, support patients as they go through difficult periods in their lives, and teach patients the skills they need to make positive behavioral changes. People dealing with mental illness; depression; anger issues; anxiety; stress; substance abuse; low self-esteem; unhealthy relationships; grief; suicidal impulses; behavioral, anxiety, or mood disorders; and post-traumatic stress, among other issues, are likely to seek the help of a mental health counselor.

Patients typically meet with a mental health counselor once or twice a week for individual and/or group counseling sessions. During counseling sessions counselors encourage patients to express their feelings and discuss whatever is troubling them. In an effort to help patients gain insights into their problems, counselors actively listen and ask nonjudgmental questions. In this way counselors

At a Glance:
Mental Health Counselor

Minimum Educational Requirements
Master's degree

Personal Qualities
Excellent listener
Ability to inspire trust

Certification and Licensing
State license

Working Conditions
Indoors

Salary Range
About $25,430 to $66,630

Number of Jobs
As of 2013 about 156,300

Future Job Outlook
Better than average

help patients deal with whatever issues they face and teach them strategies to help them cope in the future. In an interview on the website Online Counseling Degrees, mental health counselor Sha-Rhonda Davis of Hiram, Georgia, explains: "People come to you with deep problems, and they need to be able to trust that you will listen to them and do all that you can to help them help themselves. . . . It is very rewarding for me to see my clients find motivation again."

In a typical day a mental health counselor may conduct an assessment of a new patient. This involves collecting information about the patient through tests, interviews, and observation. Mental health counselors use this information to create a detailed treatment plan, which normally includes treatment goals and a timeline. Counselors also lead individual and group counseling sessions in which they teach patients alternative ways to react to stressors and/or role-play new behavioral strategies with patients. They use play therapy with troubled children in an effort to gain their confidence and get them to open up. They also confer with other professionals involved with a patient, such as physicians, social workers, probation officers, teachers, and caregivers; refer patients to social services; update patients' records; and meet with family members of a patient to advise them on how best to support the patient. Monitoring a patient's use of medication, conducting a substance abuse prevention workshop at a school or community center, and studying professional literature about new research in the field of mental health may also be part of a typical day.

Mental health counselors can specialize, limiting their practice to a specific area of mental health counseling. Or they can work with patients of all ages with a wide variety of psychological problems. Counselors in general practice are known as clinical mental health counselors. Specialized mental health counselors include child and adolescent counselors; trauma and crisis counselors; marriage, couples, and family counselors; substance abuse counselors; school counselors; and forensic counselors. Child and adolescent counselors work with troubled children and teenagers. Trauma and crisis counselors treat individuals dealing with post-traumatic stress disorder (PTSD). These individuals may include veterans, crime victims, or victims of natural disasters, among others. Marriage, couples, and family counselors help couples and families deal with emotional issues relating to divorce, death, and dysfunctional and/or abusive relationships, among other issues that impact their relationships. Substance abuse counselors treat individuals addicted to drugs and/or alcohol. School counselors assist students in schools and colleges in dealing with personal, behavioral, or academic issues. Forensic counselors combine psychology and criminology. They provide psychological support to individuals involved in the legal system. Patients include prison inmates, defendants in court trials, and law enforcement officers. Forensic counselors also provide expert testimony in criminal trials.

How Do You Become a Mental Health Counselor?

Education

To prepare for a career as a mental health counselor, high school students should take classes in psychology, health, and biology. A master's degree in counseling is required to become a mental health counselor. This typically takes two years of education beyond a bachelor's degree, or a total of six years of education beyond high school. Graduate programs in counseling admit students with any undergraduate major. However, a background in psychology, sociology, or human development is helpful. Graduate-level course work focuses on psychology, behavioral science, and counseling and includes clinical practice under the supervision of a licensed mental health counselor. Course work for specialized mental health counselors focuses on the particular specialty.

Certification and Licensing

All fifty states and the District of Columbia require that mental health counselors in private practice be licensed. Licensing requirements for mental health counselors who are not in private practice vary by state. In general, qualifications for licensing include a master's degree in counseling or psychology, successful completion of about three hundred hours of supervised clinical experience, and successful completion of a written exam. The latter may be state developed or the National Clinical Mental Health Counselor Exam (NCMHCE).

Individuals who pass the NCMHCE are eligible for national certification as clinical mental health counselors from the National Board of Certified Counselors. The board also offers specialty exams that lead to national certification in addiction and school counseling. National certification is voluntary. It is prestigious and helps counselors advance in their field.

Volunteer Work and Internships

Volunteer work and internships are a good way to gain experience in mental health counseling. Internships may also lead to permanent employment once interns have earned their license. Most universities help students find volunteer or internship positions, and most organizations seeking mental health counseling volunteers and interns provide practical training. Volunteers and interns are needed for crisis hotlines, family service agencies, rape crisis centers, alcohol and drug treatment centers, violence prevention and intervention facilities, therapeutic group homes for troubled adolescents, halfway houses, nursing homes, schools, psychiatric hospitals, correctional facilities, and youth services organizations, to name just a few possibilities. Some self-employed mental health counselors employ paid and unpaid interns. In addition, a number of international internship programs offer individuals interested in a career in counseling opportunities for unpaid internships throughout the world. In some cases participants can earn college credit for their service.

Skills and Personality

Mental health counselors should be perceptive and have excellent communication skills. They should be good listeners, observers, speakers, and writers. During a counseling session counselors must focus all their attention on the patient, listen carefully to what he or she is saying, be aware of the underlying details, ask appropriate questions, and not interrupt. Mental health counselors must also be observant of and able to read the patient's body language. Therefore, being perceptive is vital. It aids counselors in analyzing and gaining information from subtle statements and body movements patients make. And counselors should have good oral and written communication skills so that they can convey information to their patients and maintain accurate notes.

Integrity and confidentiality are other valuable character traits of mental health counselors. In order for patients to open up, they must trust the counselor and feel assured that nothing they say in a session will ever be divulged unless mandated by law. These personality traits, along with patience, compassion, and a desire to help others, assist counselors in developing a trusting relationship with patients.

Being able to stay calm, even when patients are angry or agitated, is also essential. So too is being nonjudgmental and tolerant. Counselors deal with people from diverse backgrounds. To connect with their patients they have to be sensitive to and tolerant of different cultural values. And since during counseling sessions patients often confess their worst fears and secrets, in order for treatment to succeed counselors must keep from passing judgment on their patients even if the counselor finds the patients' confessions morally offensive.

In addition, mental health counselors need to be emotionally strong. Mental health counseling is stressful. Listening to other people's problems and working with patients in crisis can take a mental and emotional toll on the listener. Although mental health counselors should be compassionate, they must be able to set boundaries and distance themselves emotionally from their patients in order to do their job effectively.

On the Job

Employers

Mental health counselors are employed by psychiatric and general hospitals, mental health and substance abuse treatment centers, outpatient care centers, residential care facilities, hospices, government agencies, nursing homes, educational institutions, private companies, correctional facilities, the offices of physicians, social advocacy organizations, and police departments, among others. Many mental health counselors are self-employed, working in solo, partnership, or group practices.

Working Conditions

Most mental health counselors work a five-day, forty-hour week. They may work evenings or weekends in order to accommodate their patients' schedules, and they may be on call for emergencies. Self-employed mental health counselors can set their own hours.

Mental health counselors usually work as part of a team. They often have to collaborate with physicians, social workers, and nurses on a patient's care. They may supervise an office staff, other counselors or interns, and social service personnel. In addition to their counseling and supervisory duties, self-employed counselors are responsible for running their businesses, which involves tasks such as billing, paying salaries, and office maintenance.

Earnings

According to the BLS, the mean average yearly earning for a mental health counselor is approximately $43,290. Salaries range from about $25,430 to $66,630, depending on the location of the job, the mental health counselor's experience, the specialty, and the type of employer. As of May 2012 the USDL reported the following average salary for mental health counselors by employer: $55,260, state government; $50,380, junior colleges; $49,230, office of other health care practitioners; $43,390, outpatient care facilities; and $43,230, psychiatric and/or substance abuse hospitals. It reports the following states with the highest mean annual wage for mental health counselors: Alaska, $56,300; Wyoming, $52,660; Arkansas, $50,590; Oregon, $50,040; and Minnesota, $49,390.

Self-employed mental health counselors do not receive employee benefits such as health insurance, paid sick and vacation days, and a retirement plan. They must provide their own benefits. Salaried mental health counselors usually receive benefits.

Opportunities for Advancement

Some mental health counselors begin their careers working for others to gain experience before opening a private practice. Mental health counselors may also advance to positions as college professors, mental health consultants, researchers, supervisors, and directors of mental health facilities. Many mental health counselors earn a doctoral degree (PhD), which helps them advance in the field.

What Is the Future Outlook for Mental Health Counselors?

The BLS predicts that employment for mental health counselors will increase by about 36 percent between 2010 and 2020. Employment for marriage and family counselors is predicted to increase by 41 percent in the same time period, which is significantly higher than the predicted 14 percent increase for all employment in the same time period. Such high employment growth is attributed to an increasing population and to the fact that insurance companies are expected to increase reimbursements to mental health counselors as an alternative to more costly psychiatrists.

Find Out More

American Association for Marriage and Family Therapy (AAMFT)
112 S. Alfred St.
Alexandria, VA 22314
phone: (703) 838-9805
website: www.aamft.org

The AAMFT is a professional organization for marriage and family counselors. It provides information on what marriage and family counselors do, marriage and family therapy topics, education, licensing and certification, continuing education, job postings, and a therapist locator.

American Counseling Association
5999 Stevenson Ave.
Alexandria, VA 22304
phone: (800) 347-6647
website: www.counseling.org

The American Counseling Association is the world's largest organization representing mental health counselors. It provides information on careers in counseling, counseling specialties, licensing and certification, mentoring programs, and job postings, and it publishes a newsletter for counselors.

American Mental Health Counselors Association (AMHCA)
801 N. Fairfax St., Suite 304
Alexandria, VA 22314
phone: (800) 362-2642
website: www.amhca.org

This organization supports and advocates for mental health counselors. It offers career information, reports news pertaining to mental health counseling, sponsors conferences, posts job openings, and provides the public with information about mental health counseling.

Council for Accreditation of Counseling and Related Educational Programs
1001 N. Fairfax St., Suite 510
Alexandria, VA 22314
phone: (703) 535-5990
website: www.cacrep.org

This organization sets standards and provides accreditation for undergraduate and graduate programs that lead to a degree in counseling. It provides a directory of accredited programs, answers questions for students interested in a career in counseling, gives licensing information, and publishes a newsletter.

Online Counseling Degrees
website: www.onlinecounselingdegrees.net

This website is geared to individuals who want to learn about a career in counseling. It offers a wealth of information about the profession, interviews with mental health counselors and students, an aptitude test, and online counseling courses.

Physical Therapist

What Does a Physical Therapist Do?

Physical therapists (PTs) work to restore or improve physical function to the greatest extent possible in people who have an illness, disability, or injury that affects their mobility. They do this through a variety of treatments that focus on building strength, flexibility, and mobility; relieving pain; and limiting physical disability. PTs design each patient's treatment plan to suit the patient's particular needs. Treatment may include therapeutic exercises; deep tissue massage; electrical stimulation; the application of hot, cold, and moist packs; and the application of ultrasound. In addition to administering treatment, PTs teach patients exercise techniques that they can practice between physical therapy sessions.

PTs work with people of all ages. Individuals with sports- or work-related injuries, back or neck injuries, sprains or fractures, stroke victims, amputees, those who have recently undergone orthopedic surgery, people with mobility and balance issues due to aging, and individuals with cerebral palsy, arthritis, congenital disorders, multiple sclerosis, osteoporosis, carpal tunnel syndrome, cardiorespiratory disease,

At a Glance:
Physical Therapist

Minimum Educational Requirements
Master's degree

Personal Qualities
Physically fit
Patient

Certification and Licensing
State license

Working Conditions
Indoors, primarily in gym-like facilities

Salary Range
About $55,620 to $112,020

Number of Jobs
As of 2013 about 185,500

Future Job Outlook
Better than average

or other medical conditions that affect movement are all likely to seek the help of a PT.

In a typical day a PT may conduct a physical assessment to determine a new patient's physical condition. Using this information the therapist designs a therapy plan unique to that patient's needs. As part of therapy, PTs may help a patient to relearn how to walk. This often involves working with patients to increase their strength and range of motion using dumbbells, exercise balls, resistance bands, stationary bikes, and other exercise equipment. Or PTs may manually move a damaged muscle through different motions. They may also administer a massage to improve muscle condition.

PTs also teach patients how to use a cane, walker, or other assistive devices and how to use and care for an artificial arm or leg. They apply an ice pack to an injured patient to reduce swelling or heat to a patient to reduce pain. Their daily work may also include consulting with other health care professionals involved in a patient's care, updating written records on patients, and supervising physical therapy assistants.

PTs can be generalists who treat a wide range of patients and mobility issues, or they can limit their practice to a specific area of physical therapy. Areas of specialization include orthopedic, pediatric, geriatric, cardiovascular and pulmonary, neurologic, and sports physical therapy. Orthopedic physical therapy is the most common specialty. Orthopedic PTs focus on treating injuries and disorders of the musculoskeletal system. Pediatric PTs work with infants, children, and teenagers with mobility issues. These young patients may have a birth defect, developmental delay, or an injury. Geriatric PTs treat the elderly, who may have problems due to weakening muscles or bones, balance disorders, joint replacements, or Alzheimer's disease, among other issues. Besides working on strengthening elderly patients, geriatric PTs focus on teaching patients alternate ways of conducting daily activities, such as safer ways to rise from a chair or ascend and descend stairs. Cardiovascular and pulmonary PTs help individuals with heart and/or lung disorders increase their endurance so that they can be more mobile. They also use special manual therapy to help patients expel excess fluid in their lungs. Neurologic PTs specialize in treating individuals with injuries and disorders of the nervous system that affect their mobility, such as cerebral palsy,

Parkinson's disease, a stroke, multiple sclerosis, traumatic brain injuries, and spinal cord injuries. Sports PTs work with athletes, sports teams, and people with sports injuries. In addition to helping rehabilitate injured individuals, these specialists focus on teaching physically active patients injury prevention and performance enhancement exercises. For instance, some PTs work with professional sports teams and elite athletes. Besides helping rehabilitate injured athletes, they teach these professionals how to safely use their muscles and joints for peak performance. In an interview with *Men's Health*, Jeff Cavaliere, a PT who trains many elite athletes, explains that he uses his knowledge of biomechanics to design training programs that challenge his competitive and ultra-fit clients.

How Do You Become a Physical Therapist?

Education

To prepare for a career as a PT, high school students should take classes in biology, health, psychology, physical education, and speech. A master's degree is required to become a PT. This typically takes about two years of education beyond a bachelor's degree, for a total of six years of education beyond high school. Some PTs earn a doctorate of physical therapy, which typically takes an additional year of study. Individuals with a bachelor's degree can enter a graduate program in physical therapy with any undergraduate major. However, most PT programs require prerequisite undergraduate courses in biology, chemistry, physiology, anatomy, physics, exercise science, and psychology. Undergraduates planning on becoming PTs should work with their academic advisers to plan their course work and major. In addition, before granting admission, many PT programs require students to have served as a volunteer or intern in a physical therapy facility.

Classes in PT programs focus on anatomy, biomechanics, neuroscience, physiology, psychology, human growth and development, and therapeutic exercises. Extensive clinical practice under the supervision of a licensed PT is an important part of the training.

Certification and Licensing

PTs must be licensed. Licensing requirements vary by state. In general, licensing requirements include graduation from an accredited physical therapy program with a master's or doctorate degree and successful completion of the National Physical Therapy Exam. Some states require passing an additional state-developed test.

Many PTs also get voluntary specialty certification offered by the American Board of Physical Therapy Specialties. To gain certification, candidates must be licensed PTs, have at least two thousand hours of clinical practice in the specialty field, and successfully complete a test in the specialty field. Having certification is prestigious and helps therapists advance in their career.

Volunteer Work and Internships

Individuals interested in a career in physical therapy are encouraged to participate in an internship and/or volunteer or work part-time in a physical therapy clinic. Doing so provides them with field experience as well as the opportunity to learn about the job by observing and assisting in patient care. A student intern at the Rusk Institute of Rehabilitation Medicine in New York describes her experience on the institute's website: "I followed a therapist as she went from patient to patient. She explained to me each patient's chart before beginning a therapy session with that patient, and taught me about certain precautions and different types of ailments related to each therapy performed. I assisted with the exercises performed by the therapist, and was shown how to evaluate the patient as well as how to record patient information in a chart."

Skills and Personality

PTs are physically active all day long. They demonstrate exercises and movement techniques to their patients, move equipment, manually manipulate and stretch muscles, lift and transfer patients, and assist patients to stand, walk, and perform other movements. These activities require strong, physically fit individuals. Not surprisingly, athletes and people who enjoy physical activity are often drawn to a career in physical therapy.

In addition, PTs should be personable and enjoy working with and helping others. Patients undergoing physical therapy are often in a lot of pain and may be tired and easily frustrated. It is not uncommon for them to want to give up. To keep patients on track and for therapy to be effective, PTs must be able to encourage and motivate frustrated patients. They need to have a positive attitude and be patient, cheerful, compassionate, determined, and firm when necessary. And because patients often take out their frustrations on their PTs, PTs need to be understanding and have thick skins. They cannot take such outpourings personally.

PTs are usually part of a larger health team. They interact with patients, patients' family members, caregivers, physicians, occupational therapists, social workers, and physical therapy assistants, among others. Being able to work on a team is an important character trait for successful PTs; so are good listening and communication skills.

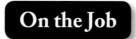

On the Job

Employers

PTs work for rehabilitation and general hospitals, long-term care facilities such as nursing homes and skilled nursing facilities, outpatient clinics, schools, the military, fitness centers, sports training facilities, home health care providers, hospices, private industry, professional sports teams, and local, state, and federal agencies such as Department of Veterans Affairs. Some PTs set up their own practices. According to the American Physical Therapy Association, 22 percent of PTs are self-employed. PTs also set up group practices with speech and occupational therapists.

Working Conditions

Most PTs work a five-day, forty-hour week, which may include evenings and/or weekends, depending on their employer. According to the USDL, 29 percent work part-time. Self-employed PTs set their own hours.

Performing tasks like transferring, lifting, and supporting patients puts PTs at risk for work-related musculoskeletal injuries and

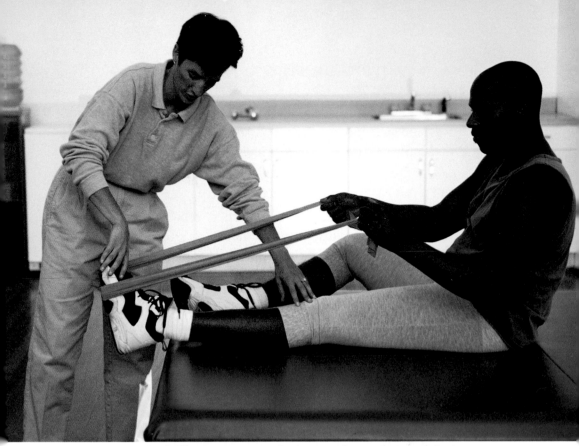

A physical therapist (PT) shows a patient the proper technique for strengthening exercises that will safely speed recovery after a sports injury. PTs also work with stroke victims, amputees, and people who have illnesses that constrain movement.

disorders, particularly of the thumb, neck, upper arms, and spine. Research shows that about 91 percent of PTs experience some sort of musculoskeletal problem during their careers. However, despite the risk of injury, according to a survey conducted by the National Opinion Research Center, PTs report one of the highest degrees of job satisfaction in the country.

Earnings

The BLS reports that the mean annual wage for PTs is $81,110, with wages ranging from about $55,620 to $112,020, depending on the location of the job, the PT's experience, the specialty, and the type of employer. The BLS further reports the following average pay for PTs by employer: $90,440, home health care agencies; $85,810, skilled nursing care facilities; $80,690, specialty hospitals; and $80,060, general hospitals. It reports the following states have the highest mean annual wage for PTs: Nevada, $110,670; Alaska, $89,950; New Jersey, $89,830; Texas, $89,790; and California, $89,370.

Self-employed PTs do not get employee benefits such as health insurance, paid sick and vacation days, and retirement benefits. Salaried PTs usually get full employee benefits.

Opportunities for Advancement

PTs working for hospitals, nursing homes, rehabilitation centers, and other health care facilities can advance to an administrative position as chief PT or director of the physical therapy department. Such positions are usually given to PTs with national certification, several years of experience, and managerial skills. PTs can also teach physical therapy at the university level. These positions usually require a national certification, several years of experience in clinical care, and a doctorate degree.

After serving as a salaried employee for a few years in order to gain experience and save money, many PTs open their own private practice or become part owner of a group practice.

What Is the Future Outlook for Physical Therapists?

According to the American Physical Therapy Association, the 2013 unemployment rate for PTs was 0.2 percent, one of the lowest rates for any occupation. This is not expected to change significantly in the future. In fact, the BLS predicts that employment for PTs will increase by 39 percent in the period from 2010 to 2020, much faster than the predicted average for all employment in the same time. The high demand for PTs is partially due to the large number of aging baby boomers (individuals born between 1946 and 1964) who are staying active longer than other generations and therefore are at risk of injury longer. Increasing longevity should also raise demand for geriatric PTs.

Find Out More

American Physical Therapy Association (APTA)
1111 N. Fairfax St.
Alexandria, VA 22314
phone: (800) 999-2782
website: www.apta.org

The APTA is a professional organization that supports and represents PTs. On its website it offers information, statistics, and a video to help educate individuals interested in a career as a PT; information about physical therapy specialties; information for prospective PT students; job postings; information about licensing; blogs; podcasts; and physical therapy news.

Federation of State Boards of Physical Therapy
124 West St. S., 3rd Floor
Alexandria, VA 22314
phone: (703) 229-3100
website: www.fsbpt.org

This organization offers information on licensing requirements and exams for all fifty states. It also provides information about the National Physical Therapy Exam, test practice material, and online exam registration. Visitors can find information about what PTs and physical therapy assistants do, the benefits of physical therapy, and how to find a licensed PT.

Owlnotes.com
website: http://owlnotes.com/interviews/27/Physical_Therapist

This website offers information about more than one hundred careers. It provides a detailed interview with a PT who describes the job, the educational requirements, a typical day, wages, pros and cons of the profession, future trends, and more.

Today in PT.com
website: www.todayinpt.com

This online magazine for PTs and people interested in the profession offers information on becoming a PT, job postings, and a blog. Visitors to the website can access numerous articles dealing with all aspects of physical therapy, many of which offer insights into what it is like to be a PT.

Radiologic Technologist

Radiologic technologists (also known as radiographers) work on the cutting edge of medical technology. They use state-of-the-art equipment to take diagnostic images of bones, tissues, organs, and vessels in the body. To get high-quality images with the right density, clarity, and detail, radiologic technologists must carefully prepare and place the patient and equipment at the correct angle and position. This takes a sharp eye and an understanding of energy, the structure of matter, measurement, and electrodynamics. It is not surprising that the American Society of Radiologic Technologists website describes the profession as "part science, part art."

In addition to taking diagnostic images, radiologic technologists are responsible for maintaining and operating the equipment and keeping records. It is up to the radiologic technologist to critique the quality of each image and redo images that are not acceptable.

At a Glance:
Radiologic Technologist

Minimum Educational Requirements
Associate's degree

Personal Qualities
Detail oriented
Good gross and fine motor skills

Certification and Licensing
State license

Working Conditions
Indoors in medical facilities

Salary Range
About $37,060 to $82,080

Number of Jobs
As of 2013 about 219,900

Future Job Outlook
Better than average

Radiologic technologists work with a variety of imaging devices. These include X-ray machines, magnetic resonance imaging (MRI) machines, computerized tomography (CT scanner) machines, ultrasound equipment, special cameras, and low-dose radioactive dyes known as radiopharmaceuticals. Radiologic technologists must be knowledgeable about radiation safety and radiation protection in order to safeguard themselves and their patients from potential hazards.

Radiologic technologists work closely with radiologists, physicians who analyze medical images in order to diagnose or rule out the possibility of injury or disease. Radiologists depend on the work of radiologic technologists to make a correct diagnosis. In fact, in many cases, such as in ultrasound images, it is the radiologic technologist's responsibility to point out abnormalities on the film for the radiologist to study.

In a typical day radiologic technologists prepare an examining room by checking that the equipment is in working order and restocking needed supplies. Once the examining room is readied, they interview the patient and record his or her medical history. They might explain the imaging procedure to be administered and then carefully position the patient—either on or near the imaging equipment. This may involve transferring patients to imaging rooms or transporting portable imaging equipment to a patient's hospital room, the emergency room, or an operating room.

Procedures done by radiologic technologists include X-raying broken bones, measuring a patient's bone density, administering a mammogram, or taking a three-dimensional image of a patient's brain. To assess the health of a fetus, radiologic technologists may run an ultrasound device over a pregnant woman's abdomen. Other procedures involve the deliverance of low doses of radioactive contrast material to patients through injection or a drink in order to detect blockages and disease. Radiologic technologists also consult with other health care professionals and work with an oncologist (a physician who specializes in cancer treatment) in planning the deliverance of radiation therapy to cancer patients.

Radiologic technologists often specialize in one or more imaging procedures. Specialty fields include medical sonography, bone densitometry, computerized tomography, cardiovascular intervention, nuclear medicine, magnetic resonance imaging, mammography, and medical dosimetry. Medical sonography technologists use ultrasound, or high-frequency sound waves, to obtain images of soft tissues, organs, blood vessels, and in pregnant women, a fetus. Medical sonography technologists can be generalists, or they can further specialize, limiting their work to taking ultrasound images of just the abdomen, nerves, eyes, heart, breast, or fetus. The images are used to detect health issues involving the different organs or to track the development and health of a fetus. Bone densitometry technologists specialize in using high-tech X-ray equipment to measure bone mineral density. The measurements are used to diagnose osteoporosis and bone loss. CT technologists specialize in using rotating X-ray devices with sophisticated computers that produce three-dimensional images of an organ's exterior and interior. The images are used to guide biopsy procedures and to detect or rule out tumors, blood clots, and brain injuries, among other conditions. Cardiovascular interventional technologists operate imaging equipment used to guide physicians in the placement of small instruments during surgical procedures involving the heart or circulatory system. Nuclear medicine technologists prepare and administer a radioactive contrast medium to patients, which they track with special cameras that produce images that physicians use to assess organ functions and diagnose blockages and blood clots. MRI technologists operate machines that use radio frequency pulses and magnetic fields to produce three-dimensional images of a body part. Mammographers use specialized X-ray equipment to produce images of the breast. These images are used to detect or rule out breast cancer. Medical dosimetrists use physics-based principles and three-dimensional computer simulations and models to pinpoint how to deliver radiation therapy to a cancerous tumor while avoiding healthy areas of the patient's body that could be harmed by radiation. They give this information to oncologists and radiation therapists who administer the treatment.

How Do You Become a Radiologic Technologist?

Education

To prepare for a career as a radiologic technologist, high school students should take classes in computer science, biology, physics, algebra, and trigonometry. Postsecondary training varies. Generally, an associate's degree from a community or technical college is required. This typically takes two years beyond high school. Some technical schools and hospitals offer one-year training programs for individuals with training in another health care field and an associate's or bachelor's degree. Prospective radiologic technologists can also enter the field with a bachelor's degree from a four-year college with an accredited program. According to the American Society of Radiologic Technologists, there are about one thousand accredited programs in the United States; most offer associate's degrees. Individuals interested in one particular specialized field of radiologic technology have the option of earning an associate's degree in that particular field, or they can earn an associate's degree in radiologic technology, which prepares them to work with basic X-ray equipment, then take additional courses in a specialty field. In this manner, they can become certified to perform a variety of procedures.

Course work toward certification as a radiologic technologist includes classes in anatomy, biology, physics, radiation safety, computer science, medical terminology, communications, radiographic equipment, radiographic procedures, patient care, and medical laws and ethics. Hands-on laboratory classes teach students positioning skills. Training also includes clinical practice under the supervision of a certified radiologic technologist.

Certification and Licensing

Most states require that radiologic technologists be licensed. Licensing requirements vary. Generally, candidates must hold a minimum of an associate's degree from an accredited program and pass a licensing exam. Thirty states use an exam developed and administered by the American Registry of Radiological Technologists (ARRT). Passing this exam is also a requirement for certification, which, while voluntary, indicates that the individual has met certain standards within the profession. Certification is helpful in gaining employment. The ARRT offers primary certification in radiologic technology (radiography), nuclear medicine technology, and sonography. Once an individual holds ARRT certification in any of these fields, he or she can get additional certification from the ARRT in mammography, computerized tomography, bone densitometry, and cardiac interventional radiography. Certification in medical dosimetry can be obtained through the Medical Dosimetrist Certification Board.

Volunteer Work and Internships

Individuals interested in a career as a radiologic technologist can learn more about the profession by volunteering in a hospital, nursing home, imaging facility, or a physician's office that employs an imaging professional. Getting a part-time job in any of these facilities also gives individuals a chance to interact with radiologic technologists. Another option for prospective radiologic technologists is to shadow a radiologic technologist for at least a day to get a sense of the true nature of the work and see if the profession is right for them.

Skills and Personality

In order to see small details at close range and operate complex equipment effectively, radiologic technologists should have good eyesight, manual dexterity, arm-hand steadiness, and eye-hand coordination. These traits are vital for taking high-quality images. Radiologic technologists should also be strong and fit. They must position patients; turn, lift, and transfer patients who are unable to perform these actions without assistance; move heavy portable equipment; and stand on their feet for hours at a time.

Radiologic technologists also need good communication skills so that they can explain procedures to patients and answer patients' questions. Often patients are nervous or scared about a procedure, or they may be sick or in pain. Being personable, patient, and compassionate helps put patients at their ease. When patients feel reassured, they are more likely to maintain the appropriate position while the radiologic technology is scanning their body.

Additional skills include being mathematical, analytical, organized, detail oriented, and computer literate. Indeed, radiologic technologists should be proficient in and enjoy using computers and technologically sophisticated equipment. And since radiologic technologists usually work as part of a health care team, the ability to work well in a team setting and take directions from physicians is essential.

On the Job

Employers

The majority of radiologic technologists work in hospital radiology departments. They are also employed by diagnostic laboratories, the offices of physicians, nursing homes, cancer care and treatment centers, outpatient facilities, the military, and public health facilities. Some radiologic technologists are employed by educational institutions or international health organizations as teachers of radiologic technology.

Working Conditions

Most radiologic technologists work a five-day, forty-hour week. However, their work hours often include evenings, weekends, and on-call hours. Some radiologic technologists work twelve-hour alternating shifts with three or four days off per week. Opportunities for part-time work are also an option.

Radiologic technologists face a risk of exposure to radiation. However, the risk is minimized by wearing lead gloves and aprons and other protective shielding devices and by instruments that monitor radiation exposure. Radiologic technologists wear badges that measure radiation levels in the radiation area. Detailed records are kept on their cumulative lifetime dose to protect them from overexposure.

Earnings

The BLS reports that average wages for a radiologic technologist range from $37,060 to $82,080, with an average annual mean salary of $54,620. Average annual mean wages are highest in the following states: Massachusetts, $82,080; California, $70,590; Alaska, $67,980; Hawaii, $66,610. Radiologic technologists with specialty certification usually earn more. According to the BLS, the average wages for nuclear medicine technologists range from $50,560 to $93,320, with an average annual mean salary of $70,180. The BLS also reports that the average annual wage for a sonographer ranges from $43,990 to $85,950, with an average annual mean salary of $63,010. Salary.com reports that the average annual salary for a medical dosimetrist ranges from $85,452 to $118,064, with an average annual mean salary of $100,637. All types of radiologic technologists usually receive benefits such as health insurance, paid vacation and sick days, and retirement benefits.

Opportunities for Advancement

Radiologic technologists can gain certification in any number of specialized areas, which makes them highly regarded multiskilled professionals and provides them with opportunities for advancement.

Radiologic technologists with at least five years of clinical experience can advance to an administrative position such as shift supervisor, chief radiologic technologist, or director of imaging. These jobs involve directing personnel, ordering equipment, and often, planning budgets. They can also become classroom and/or clinical instructors in radiology training programs or work as researchers developing new and better imaging strategies and radiation treatments. For example, some nuclear medical technologists research the effects of different levels of radiation on the various organs of the body, including the brain. Radiologic technologists can also move into positions in sales, selling imaging equipment to medical facilities.

Radiologic technologists who earn a bachelor's degree can become radiologic extenders (also known as radiologist assistants). Radiologic extenders work as assistants to radiologists. They assess and educate patients, evaluate images, order follow-up images, and perform a variety of interventional procedures involving radiopharmaceuticals.

What Is the Future Outlook for Radiologic Technologists?

The BLS predicts that employment for radiologic technologists will increase by 28 percent in the period from 2010 to 2020, much faster than the predicted average for all employment in the same time period. The high demand for radiologic technologists is attributed to a growing and aging population and to a growing emphasis on detecting disease early.

Find Out More

American Association of Medical Dosimetrists
2201 Cooperative Way, Suite 600
Herndon, VA 20171
phone: (703) 677-8701
website: www.medicaldosimetry.org

This organization represents medical dosimetrists. It offers information about the profession, a listing of accredited programs, job postings, continuing education opportunities, and publications. The website's home page has links to more about the profession.

American Institute of Ultrasound in Medicine
14750 Sweitzer Ln., Suite 100
Laurel, MD 20707
phone: (301) 498-4100
website: www.aium.org

This organization is dedicated to advancing the use of ultrasound in medicine. Visitors to its website can access lots of information about a career as a sonographer. The website also has job postings, medical news, continuing education opportunities, accreditation information, and access to a journal the organization publishes.

American Society of Radiologic Technologists (ASRT)
15000 Central Ave. SE
Albuquerque, NM 87213
phone: (800) 444-2778
website: www.asrt.org

The ASRT is a professional organization for general radiologic technologists and specialists. It provides a wealth of information about careers in radiology, certification, continuing education, and job postings. It offers video interviews with radiologic technologists on its website. The society also publishes a newsletter, magazine, and professional journal.

Society of Nuclear Medicine and Molecular Imaging
1850 Samuel Morse Dr.
Reston, VA 20190
phone: (703) 708-9000
website: www.snm.org

This organization offers information about nuclear medicine. Visitors can access articles, pamphlets, and a video about nuclear medicine and careers in nuclear medical technology. The organization also offers job postings, research news, professional publications, continuing education opportunities, and information about grants, fellowships, and scholarships.

Registered Nurse

What Does a Registered Nurse Do?

Registered nurses (RNs) care for people who are ill or injured. They usually work more closely with patients and their families than any other health care professional. They implement patients' treatment based on physicians' orders; record and evaluate the effectiveness of the treatment and the patients' progress; provide emotional support for patients and their families; and educate patients, families, and communities about healthy practices.

Although no two days are the same for an RN, in a typical day an RN may consult with a physician about a patient's diagnosis, treatment, and progress. Then, throughout the day, the RN monitors the patient, performing tasks such as taking the patient's vital signs and administering medication. RNs also prepare patients for and assist during surgery. They help deliver babies, educate new parents about caring for their baby, and care for premature infants in neonatal intensive care units. They change dressings, operate sophisticated medical equipment, and insert feeding tubes and catheters into patients. Providing care for wounded troops, treating schoolchildren with minor injuries and illnesses,

At a Glance:
Registered Nurse

Minimum Educational Requirements
Associate's degree

Personal Qualities
Calm under pressure
Detail oriented

Certification and Licensing
State license

Working Conditions
Indoor, primarily in health care facilities

Salary Range
About $45,040 to $122,990

Number of Jobs
As of 2013 about 2.6 million

Future Job Outlook
Better than average

48

and administering flu shots to the public may also be part of an RN's day. In addition, RNs prepare patients for discharge from the hospital, instruct patients and their families about how to deal with a long-term health condition, direct other nurses and nurse's aides, instruct student nurses, visit the home of a sick patient, and provide emergency care in a factory or business setting.

Besides providing medical care, RNs also provide emotional care and support to patients and their families. For instance, one hospice nurse tries to joke around with his patients while examining them. This cheers the patients up. The same nurse spends time with his patients' families, helping them understand exactly what is going on with their loved one and what might happen in the future. This helps them cope better. As Baltimore critical care nurse Kevin M. explains in an interview on the Discover Nursing website: "What we do affects people's lives in a significant way."

Like physicians, RNs can specialize in different types of nursing. There are more than one hundred different fields of specialization, and RNs can have more than one specialty field. Some areas of specialization are determined by the RNs workplace, such as school nurses, who work in school health clinics; surgical nurses, who work in operating rooms; critical care nurses, who work in intensive care units; emergency room nurses, who work in hospital emergency rooms; hospice nurses, who work with terminally ill patients in hospice care; or occupational nurses, who work in factories or businesses, to name a few. Other specialties are defined by the body part or the type of patients RNs treat, such as dialysis nurses, who work with patients with kidney failure; oncology nurses, who work with cancer patients; geriatrics nurses, who work with the elderly; or neonatal nurses, who work with newborn infants.

How Do You Become a Registered Nurse?

Education

To prepare for a career as an RN, high school students should take classes in biology, chemistry, math, and speech. After high school, prospective RNs can follow one of three different educational paths.

They can earn an associate's degree in nursing from a community college. This generally requires two years of postsecondary education. They can attend a three-year diploma program offered by hospitals and training schools. Or they can earn a bachelor's of science degree in nursing from a college or university. This usually takes four years of postsecondary education. A bachelor's degree helps nurses advance in the field and prepares them for administrative positions. According to the BLS, many RNs earn an associate's degree or a diploma in nursing. Once employed in a health care setting they work toward a bachelor's degree with the help of tuition reimbursement benefits, which many employers offer as an employee benefit.

Acceptance into all three types of programs can be quite competitive. In many cases, to gain admittance aspiring nurses must successfully complete an entry exam and have a strong grade point average. Nursing school course work includes classes in anatomy, physiology, psychology, microbiology, chemistry, nutrition, social sciences, math, and nursing concepts and techniques. All programs include intensive supervised clinical practice in a wide range of specialty areas.

Certification and Licensing

All fifty states and the District of Columbia require RNs be licensed. To become licensed, RNs must graduate from an accredited nursing program and successfully complete a written exam administered by the National Council of State Boards of Nursing.

RNs can also obtain certification in more than thirty specialty areas. Certification requirements include successful completion of a written exam and postgraduate training in the area of specialization. Many RNs hold multiple certifications. Certification is prestigious, indicating that an RN has achieved mastery in the field. Certification helps RNs advance in their profession and raises their earning potential.

Volunteer Work and Internships

Individuals interested in a career in nursing can learn about the profession and experience what it is like to work with patients by volunteering in a hospital or other medical facility. Most hospitals train and supervise volunteers. Some hospitals offer a tuition reimbursement program for volunteers currently attending nursing school, if the nursing student agrees to work for the hospital as a salaried RN after licensure. Volunteer positions are also available with the Red Cross for nursing school students.

A number of private companies and international organizations offer opportunities for high school and nursing school students to volunteer in medical facilities throughout the world. Many of these organizations also offer unpaid international internship programs for nursing students with college credit. Typically, international volunteers and interns must pay for their own transportation. Some, but not all, international programs charge tuition.

Skills and Personality

Being an RN is physically and mentally challenging. RNs are always on the go. They have to lift heavy objects and patients, stand for long periods of time, bend, stretch, and twist repeatedly, and work long shifts. They need to be physically strong, energetic, and hardworking to do their job effectively. RNs must also be emotionally strong. They encounter many traumatic and stressful situations and witness pain and suffering on a daily basis. Although RNs should be empathetic, they have to be able to accept death and suffering without allowing it to affect them personally. Similarly, they must be tough enough to administer painful treatments. Nurses who become overwhelmed with emotion each time they witness suffering or death cannot do their job. Counterbalancing their toughness, RNs should also be compassionate, patient, and calm. These traits comfort sick and frightened patients and give them moral support.

Being alert and detail oriented is also vital. RNs must pay careful attention to everything they do; even a small error can have dire consequences. They also must be alert and observant of their patients so that they can anticipate, detect, and treat their patients' spoken and unspoken needs. RNs should also be decisive and good problem solvers. When a patient takes a turn for the worse, nurses are usually the first health care professionals on the scene. Their ability to solve problems, make rapid decisions, and act quickly can make the difference between life and death.

Having good communication skills is another important skill RNs need. Nurses must be able to follow physicians' orders without any problem and communicate effectively with their patients and their patients' families. RNs serve as an advocate for patients and a link between patients and physicians. They must be able to convey patient information successfully to physicians and other health care professionals.

Employers

According to the BLS, 48 percent of all RNs in the United States are employed by hospitals. RNs are also employed in a number of other settings such as nursing homes, hospices, educational institutions, physicians' private practices, outpatient clinics, rehabilitation facilities, home health care agencies, public health agencies, correctional facilities, summer camps, the military, private businesses and industrial facilities, and in the homes of private patients. Some RNs work for nursing staffing agencies as traveling nurses. They travel (free of charge) to different locations throughout the United States to fill temporary staffing shortages in hospitals. This gives them the opportunity to see many different places.

Working Conditions

The BLS reports that 80 percent of all RNs work full-time. Those who work in educational institutions, public health agencies, physician's offices, private businesses, or industrial facilities usually work a standard five-day, forty-hour workweek. Those who work in hospitals and other round-the-clock health care facilities usually work eight- to twelve-hour rotating shifts. They may work three or four days per week, including nights, weekends, and holidays, and be on call. When medical facilities are short-handed, RNs often work double shifts, which can mean working sixteen to twenty-four hours in one day, and more than forty hours per week. Options for seasonal, temporary, and part-time work are also available.

RNs are on their feet most of the time. They lift and transfer patients, which puts them at risk for back, neck, and shoulder injuries. According to the American Nursing Association, in 2011, 56 percent of RNs who responded to a survey reported experiencing musculoskeletal pain caused or made worse by their work. Fatigue related to working long hours, inadequate staffing due to shortages of qualified RNs, exposure to infectious diseases, needle sticks, and the physical and emotional challenges of nursing also stress an RN's health. To ward off infection, RNs wear masks and gloves, wash their hands often, and follow strict guidelines in handling needles to protect themselves from needle pricks.

RNs are also at risk of on-the-job assault by distraught or mentally unbalanced patients and/or their family members. The American Nursing Association reports that in 2011, 34 percent of RNs responding to a survey ranked on-the-job assaults in their top three safety concerns.

Earnings

According to the BLS, yearly wages for RNs range from about $45,040 to $122,990, depending on the location of the job and the RN's experience, education, and certifications. It reports the mean average salary to be $67,930. Average mean wages are highest in the following states: California, $94,120; Hawaii, $84,750; Massachusetts, $83,370; Alaska, $80,970; and Oregon, $78,530.

RNs usually receive paid benefits, including health insurance, paid sick and vacation days, and retirement benefits. Some hospitals offer RNs a monetary sign-on bonus when they are first hired and paid college tuition if they want to advance their education.

Opportunities for Advancement

RNs have many opportunities to advance in the profession. They can move up from a staff nurse to a head nurse and from a head nurse to a nursing administrator and/or the chief of nursing. RNs who earn a master's degree and specialized certification can become advanced practice nurses. Advanced practice nurses include nurse-midwives, nurses who care for pregnant women and deliver babies; nurse anesthetists, nurses who administer anesthesia to surgical patients; clinical nurse specialists, clinical care nurses valued for their expertise; and nurse practitioners, nurses who can diagnose and treat minor illnesses much like a physician. Since advanced practice nurses are entrusted with more responsibility than RNs, their wages are higher. As an example, the American Academy of Nurse Practitioners reports that the annual mean wage of a nurse practitioner is about $89,450.

RNs with advanced degrees can also become college instructors, go into research or pharmaceutical sales, or serve as consultants for drug manufacturers or insurance companies.

What Is the Future Outlook for RNs?

RNs are the largest group employed by the health care industry. Yet there are shortages of RNs in some parts of the country, and the demand for RNs is expected to increase in the future. The BLS predicts that employment for RNs will increase by 26 percent between 2010 and 2020. Top employment opportunities for nurses are predicted to be in physicians' offices, with an increase of 48 percent through 2018.

Find Out More

American Association of Colleges of Nursing (AACN)
1 Dupont Circle NW, Suite 530
Washington, DC 20036
phone: (202) 463-6930
website: www.aacn.nche.edu

This association provides information about a career in nursing, accredited nursing programs, scholarships, financial aid, licensing and certification, and employment prospects.

American Nurses Association (ANA)
8515 Georgia Ave., Suite 400
Silver Springs, MD 20910
phone: (800) 274-4262
website: www.nursingworld.org

The ANA is the largest nursing association in the United States. Its website offers a wealth of information on a career in nursing, nursing specialties, licensing and certification, nursing news, continuing education for nurses, and nursing publications.

Discover Nursing
phone: (888) 981-9111
website: www.discovernursing.com

This website sponsored by Johnson & Johnson is dedicated to recruiting people into the nursing profession. It offers a wealth of material about nursing careers, nursing schools and scholarships, nursing specialties, the future outlook for nurses, interviews with nurses, and free publications.

National League for Nursing
61 Broadway, 33rd Floor
New York, NY 10006
phone: (800) 669-1656
website: www.nln.org

This organization of nurses provides information for both practicing and aspiring nurses. The website has links to other websites offering information about a career in nursing. The organization also provides information about finding accredited nursing programs and financial aid, licensing and certification exams, and industry news.

Respiratory Therapist

What Does a Respiratory Therapist Do?

Breathing is an activity that most people take for granted. Yet many people have health issues that make it difficult for them to breathe. Respiratory therapists (RTs) save lives every day by diagnosing and treating individuals with respiratory and cardiopulmonary (heart-lung) problems. Using a variety of medical equipment and medications, RTs provide therapy that helps patients improve their ability to breathe. An RT's patients include premature infants, whose lungs are not fully developed; children; and adults of all ages. These individuals may be suffering from disorders like emphysema, asthma, bronchitis, pneumonia, heart disease, stroke, sleep apnea, cystic fibrosis, chronic obstructive pulmonary disease, or other conditions that affect breathing. They may also be victims of accidents, shock, burns, violent crimes, drowning, electric shock, or a drug overdose, among other possibilities.

In a typical day an RT may interview patients, perform chest exams, and administer tests that measure how a patient's lungs and circulatory system are working. As part of these tests an RT may draw an arterial blood sample from a patient in order to assess the level of oxygen and

At a Glance:

Respiratory Therapist

Minimum Educational Requirements

Associate's degree

Personal Qualities

Good problem-solving skills
Manual dexterity

Certification and Licensing

State license

Working Conditions

Indoors in health care facilities

Salary Range

About $40,980 to $75,430

Number of Jobs

As of 2013 about 112,700

Future Job Outlook

Better than average

carbon dioxide in the patient's bloodstream. Administering inhalant medication, teaching a patient the best way to inhale medication to ensure its effectiveness, and developing and implementing a care plan for a patient with a chronic breathing disorder are also parts of an average day. So are monitoring and treating a patient with respiratory issues during medical transport and monitoring a patient's breathing during surgery. When patients cannot breathe on their own, RTs are responsible for inserting a breathing tube into the patient's windpipe, connecting the breathing tube to an artificial breathing machine known as a mechanical ventilator, and setting the rate, concentration, and volume of oxygen that the ventilator delivers into the patient's lungs. In addition to treating patients with ventilators and other equipment, RTs check breathing devices such as ventilators, oxygen masks, and oxygen tanks for mechanical problems. RTs also have other duties that fill their day. They often administer emergency care such as artificial respiration and external heart massage to a heart attack victim, drain fluid from patients' lungs, confer with physicians and other health care professionals about a patient's treatment, supervise respiratory technicians, and maintain records of a patient's therapy and progress.

How Do You Become an RT?

Education

To prepare for a career as an RT high school students should take classes in biology, chemistry, physics, and math. As the USDL explains: "Respiratory care involves basic mathematical problem solving and an understanding of chemical and physical principles. For example, respiratory care workers must be able to compute medication dosages and calculate gas concentrations."

High school graduates have two options to train for a career as an RT. They can earn an associate's degree from an accredited respiratory therapy program at a community college or technical institute, which typically takes two years of postsecondary training. RTs can also enter the field with a bachelor's degree in an accredited respiratory therapy program from a four-year college. Having a bachelor's degree is an indication of a higher level of expertise and helps RTs advance in the field.

Course work includes classes in physiology, anatomy, biology, chemistry, pharmacology, psychology, anesthesiology, cardiovascular and respiratory diseases, as well as hands-on instruction in respiratory therapy techniques. The last includes pulmonary function testing, blood-gas analysis, mechanical ventilation, and airway management. Both programs require extensive supervised clinical practice.

Certification and Licensing

All states except Alaska and Hawaii require that RTs be certified. To gain certification, candidates must graduate with a minimum of an associate's degree from an accredited respiratory therapy program and successfully complete an exam administered by the National Board for Respiratory Care (NBRC). Certified respiratory therapists (CRTs) can voluntarily become registered respiratory therapist (RRTs) by successfully completing the RRT exam, which is also administered by the NBRC. Doing so demonstrates an exceptional level of competency and helps RTs advance in the profession.

In addition, RRTs can acquire specialty credentials in three areas: neonatal pediatrics, which demonstrates excellence in working with premature infants; sleep, which demonstrates excellence in working with people with sleep apnea or other sleep disorders that affect breathing; and adult critical care, which demonstrates excellence in working with intensive care patients. Having specialty certification helps RRTs advance in the profession and earn higher wages. According to the American Association for Respiratory Care, "Employers as well as patients want to know their caregivers are competent. Specialty credentials are one way to demonstrate a distinct level of professionalism and competence to these groups."

Volunteer Work and Internships

Many hospitals and long-term care facilities have programs in which individuals interested in pursuing a career in respiratory therapy can shadow an RT for one day to a month. This gives aspiring RTs a chance to observe firsthand what the job entails and decide whether it is the best career choice for them.

Young people, in some cases as young as fourteen, can also volunteer in the respiratory department of a hospital or other health care facility. Volunteers do not usually work with patients; they typically greet patients, answer phones, and assist in the preparation and distribution of educational material. However, since volunteers usually come into contact with RTs and RT students doing clinical practice, they have an opportunity to witness and learn about RT training.

Skills and Personality

It takes a variety of skills and mental and physical traits to be a successful RT. For example, RTs should have an aptitude for mechanics, have a steady hand, good eye-hand coordination, and good eyesight. These skills help them assemble and operate small and large equipment that helps patients breathe, make quick and accurate adjustments to the equipment, watch gauges and other indicators to ensure the equipment is working properly, and use the equipment with precision. RTs should also be physically fit. They spend much of their working hours standing and may have to lift and/or transfer patients and equipment. And since RTs treat many critically ill patients, they need to be emotionally strong. Although RTs should be compassionate and caring, in order to do their job effectively they cannot take a patient's suffering or death personally.

Being calm, no matter the situation, is also vital. RTs deal with medical emergencies on a daily basis. Having a calm demeanor helps comfort distraught or frightened patients and their families, which makes it easier to treat them. Being able to think and act quickly and make rapid decisions during a crisis are other key traits. Having excellent critical-thinking and problem-solving skills helps make this possible. RTs should also be organized and detail oriented. There is little room for mistakes in respiratory care, so RTs must be precise in every aspect of their work. This includes patient care, equipment care and maintenance, and maintaining and updating patients' records.

RTs work independently and as part of a health care team. They therefore must be able to function as a part of a group and follow physicians' orders, while also being responsive to each patient's needs and adjusting treatment accordingly. They need good communication and listening skills so that they can actively listen to their patients and understand the points being made; clearly explain procedures to patients and their families; answer their questions; and instruct patients with chronic illnesses on the use of breathing devices. Good communication skills also allow RTs to share information about a patient with the attending physician and other members of the health care team.

On the Job

Employers

According to Explore Health Careers.org, about 75 percent of RTs are employed by hospitals. RTs are also employed by sleep disorder clinics, long-term care facilities, home health care agencies, rehabilitation facilities, diagnostic laboratories, physician's private practices, specialized respiratory therapy clinics, the military, and patient transport agencies. Some RTs work for manufacturers of medical breathing devices or for companies that rent such devices to patients to use in their homes. RRTs with a bachelor's degree and clinical work experience may also be employed by educational institutions as instructors in RT programs.

Working Conditions

Most RTs work a forty-hour week, consisting of rotating twelve-hour shifts with three or four days off per week. Working double shifts is not uncommon. RTs are usually on call and often work nights, weekends, and holidays. They spend long periods standing on their feet and often have to lift and transfer patients. They are therefore at risk of back, shoulder, and neck injuries. RTs also face many emergency situations, which can cause them emotional stress.

RTs use gases that are stored under pressure in treating patients. Working around gases stored under pressure can be hazardous. RTs are trained to maintain and test their equipment and to take specific safety precautions, which minimizes their risk of injury. RTs are also exposed to infectious diseases. Wearing surgical gloves and masks and practicing frequent hand washing helps lessen an RT's risk of infection.

Earnings

The BLS reports that the average annual wage for an RT ranges from $40,980 to $75,430, depending on the location of the job and the RT's level of experience and credentials. It reports a mean average annual salary of $55,870. According to the BLS, average mean annual wages are highest in the following states: California, $73,320; Nevada, $69,540; Connecticut, $67,890; New Jersey, $67,670; and Alaska, $67,220. Most RTs receive employee benefits that include health insurance, paid sick and vacation days, and retirement benefits.

Opportunities for Advancement

Becoming an RRT helps RTs advance in the profession. Having specialty credentials helps RRTs to advance even further and puts them at the top of the pay schedule. RRTs with a bachelor's or a master's degree and clinical experience can advance to an administrative position as head of the respiratory therapy department of a hospital or other health care facility or the branch manager of a home health care agency. Possessing at least a bachelor's degree and clinical experience also allows RTs to advance to faculty positions in respiratory therapy training programs in community colleges and universities. Some RTs move to research, development, and/or sales, using their knowledge of respiratory care to develop and market medications and medical devices used for respiratory care. Some RTs branch off into smoking cessation counseling. Others go into business for themselves, opening private practice respiratory care clinics.

What Is the Future Outlook for RTs?

The BLS predicts that employment for RTs will increase by 28 percent in the period from 2010 to 2020, much faster than the predicted average for all employment in the same time period. The high demand for RTs is attributed to a growing and aging population. Older individuals are at greater risk of contracting pneumonia, heart disease, emphysema, and chronic bronchitis, which increases their need for respiratory care. At the same time, the increasing survival rate of premature infants, many of whom depend on a ventilator, and the increasing incidence of asthma in children further raise the need for RTs.

Find Out More

American Association for Respiratory Care (AARC)
9425 N. McArthur Blvd., Suite 100
Irving, TX 75063
phone: (972) 243-2272
website: www.aarc.org

The AARC is a professional organization of RTs. It provides information about a career in respiratory therapy, education and training, credentialing, credentialing test preparation, and specialty fields. It also provides job postings, professional news, webcasts, networking opportunities, and career advice.

Commission on Accreditation for Respiratory Care (COARC)
1248 Harwood Rd.
Bedford, TX 76021
phone: (817) 283-2835
website: www.coarc.com

The COARC assesses and accredits respiratory therapy training programs. It provides information on the importance of enrolling in an accredited program and a list of all accredited respiratory therapy programs in the United States.

Explore Health Careers.org
website: http://explorehealthcareers.org/en/Career/23/Respiratory_Therapist

Explore Health Careers.org is a website dedicated to providing information about health care careers. The section on a career as an RT provides an overview of the profession and information about training, education, and wages.

National Board for Respiratory Care (NBRC)
8310 Nieman Rd.
Lenexa, KS 66214
phone: (913) 895-4900
website: www.nbrc.org

The NBRC is a national board that tests and certifies RTs. It provides information about CRT, RRT, and specialty credentialing and exams and a listing of all accredited respiratory therapy training programs in the United States.

Surgeon

Surgeons are specialized physicians who diagnose and treat injuries, diseases, and physical deformities through surgery. Surgery involves making an incision on a patient's body, opening the body up to uncover the problem, diagnosing and, hopefully, repairing or removing the problem, then closing the incision. Using their own two hands, surgeons make immediate and long-lasting changes in patients' lives. For instance, when a New York woman who was pregnant with triplets developed a life-threatening tear in the main artery to her heart, surgeons saved four lives at one time. Performing dual procedures in one operating room, they successfully delivered the premature babies, then performed open-heart surgery on the mother. To do their job, surgeons use traditional medical tools as well as cutting-edge medical technology like robotic surgical equipment, computers, three-dimensional imagery, and laser devices. Surgeons are the leaders of a medical team that includes RNs, surgical assistants, and an anesthesiologist, among others.

In addition to performing surgery, surgeons hold pre- and postsurgery consultations with patients. Typically, surgeons reserve one or two days per week

At a Glance:

Surgeon

Minimum Educational Requirements
Doctorate of medicine (MD) or a doctorate of osteopathy (DO)

Personal Qualities
Good eye-hand coordination
Decisive

Certification and Licensing
State license

Working Conditions
Indoors in a clean, sterile environment

Salary Range
About $117, 390 to $656, 250

Number of Jobs
As of 2013 about 135,900

Future Jobs Outlook
Better than average

for just this purpose. During presurgery consultations, surgeons examine the patient, discuss treatment options, and if surgery is an option, explain the surgical procedure and the possible risks and benefits of surgery. During postsurgical consultations, surgeons monitor the patient's progress. Surgeons must maintain careful records on each patient's diagnosis, treatment, and progress throughout.

Although no two days are the same for a surgeon, in a typical day, depending on a surgeon's specialty, a surgeon may stop uncontrollable bleeding, reattach a severed finger, repair a broken bone, or reshape the face of a burn victim. Surgeons may repair a hernia using laparoscopic surgery. Laparoscopic surgery is a minimally invasive procedure that uses special instruments, computers, and other high-tech equipment. Removing part of a cancerous colon, then reconnecting the remaining colon segments with medical staples may also be a part of a surgeon's day. Other activities include studying a CT scan of a patient's internal organs, consulting with other health care professionals, and meeting with a patient's family after surgery to discuss the patient's condition.

There are many types of surgeons with a wide range of specialties. General surgeons, physicians who perform surgery on almost all parts of the body, comprise the largest surgical specialty. Thoracic surgeons are another specialty; they provide surgical care for medical conditions in the chest, including the heart and lungs. Colon and rectal surgeons deal with conditions involving the intestines, rectum, and anus. Vascular surgeons specialize in surgery involving the blood vessels. Obstetrics and gynecology surgeons perform cesarean sections in order to surgically deliver babies. They also provide surgical care to fetuses and to the female reproductive system, whereas pediatric surgeons limit their practice to the surgical treatment of children. Neurological surgeons focus on treatment of the nervous system, including the brain and spinal cord; ophthalmic surgeons specialize in surgical treatment of the eyes. Orthopedic surgeons are another common specialty. They surgically treat bones and muscles. Plastic surgeons perform surgery involving the skin and underlying areas. Surgeons who specialize in removing and replacing damaged organs with healthy organs are known as transplant surgeons. Other specialists known as trauma surgeons treat physical injuries in an emergency setting.

How Do You Become a Surgeon?

Education

Becoming a surgeon involves a lot of training. To prepare for a career as a surgeon, high school students should take classes in biology, chemistry, physics, and math. Postsecondary aspiring surgeons must obtain a bachelor's degree, which usually takes four years. Then they must attend medical school for an additional four years. Upon graduation from medical school, aspiring surgeons must complete a surgical residency program in which they work in a hospital treating surgical patients under the supervision of experienced surgeons. Depending on the surgical specialty, residency programs can last from three to eight years.

Admittance to medical school is highly competitive. There are two types of medical schools: allopathic medical school, which confers a doctorate of medicine (MD), and osteopathic medical school, which confers a doctorate of osteopathy (DO). Graduates of both types of medical schools can go on to become surgeons. To enter medical school, aspiring surgeons must submit their undergraduate transcripts, letters of recommendation, and their scores from the medical college admission test (MCAT), among other admission criteria. While medical schools do not require a particular college major, prerequisite classes for medical school admission typically include two semesters of biology, two semesters of chemistry, one semester of organic chemistry, one semester of biochemistry, and one year of physics, along with associated laboratory exercises. Therefore, a science-related major helps prepare aspiring surgeons for medical school.

Medical school course work is challenging. According to the Association of Medical Colleges, the first two years consist of classes in biochemistry, biology, genetics, anatomy, the organ system, neuroscience, immunology, pathology, pharmacology, infectious diseases, medical law, and clinical diagnoses and treatments. In the final two years students become part of a medical team and rotate through different medical specialties. This gives students the opportunity to decide which specialty area they want to practice. Once prospective surgeons graduate from medical school they begin their surgical residency in their chosen surgical specialty. Surgical residents work in

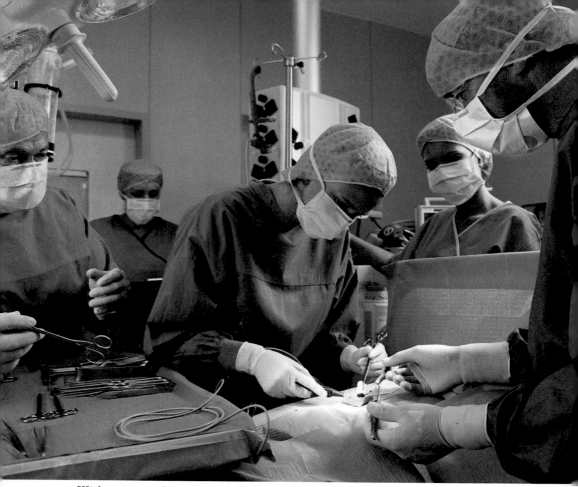

With assistance from nurses and other medical specialists, a surgeon operates on a patient. The work of the surgeon requires technical knowledge, confidence, and the ability to critically assess unexpected complications.

hospitals and treat patients under the supervision of a practicing surgeon. Depending on the surgical specialty, the residency program can last up to eight years. In contrast, the residency program for family practice physicians, pediatricians, and internal medicine physicians, for example, lasts three years.

Certification and Licensing

All fifty states and the District of Columbia require that surgeons be licensed. To become licensed, candidates must graduate from an accredited medical school, successfully complete a residency program, and pass the US Medical Licensing Examination or the Comprehensive Osteopathic Medical Licensing Examination. Licensed surgeons can obtain voluntary certification from the American Board of Surgery in general surgery, pediatric surgery, vascular surgery, surgical critical care, surgical oncology (cancer surgery), or hand surgery by completing at least five years of residency training and successfully completing a written and oral exam. Surgeons in other specialties can obtain certification from other specialty boards such as the American Board of Orthopedic Surgery, the American Board of Neurological Surgery, the American Board of Plastic Surgery, and the American Board of Thoracic Surgery in a similar manner. Certification is prestigious, indicating that a surgeon has achieved mastery in the field.

Volunteer Work and Internships

Individuals interested in a career as a surgeon can learn about the profession and experience what it is like to work with patients by volunteering in a hospital. Most hospitals train and supervise volunteers. Aspiring surgeons can also arrange to shadow a surgeon as the physician does hospital rounds and holds pre- and postsurgery consultations with patients. Nonmedical personnel are not admitted into the operating theater.

To prepare college students for medical school, the Robert Wood Johnson Foundation sponsors a free six-week summer medical program at twelve sites across the United States. The program provides participants with academic enrichment in science topics relevant to a medical career, study skills development, job-shadowing experience, and clinical experience in hospitals or other health care facilities. There is no charge for travel or room and board. Interested individuals must apply to the program, and acceptance is based on many factors, including grade point average and a personal essay.

Other organizations offer high school and college students an opportunity to participate in medically oriented summer programs in hospitals and clinics throughout the world. In most cases participants pay a set fee that covers their room and board, hospital placement, and clinical training. Transportation is extra. Some programs offer participants college credit. In addition, organizations such as Doctors Without Borders offer paid internships in their offices in the United States. These positions are competitive and often require a bachelor's degree.

Skills and Personality

Surgery is physical labor. A complex operation can last ten or more hours. Surgeons must stand for long periods; make fast, repetitive movements involving their hands, fingers, and wrists; and bend, twist, reach, and stretch repeatedly. They must have strong, flexible bodies, steady hands, good eyesight, good eye-hand coordination, and excellent manual dexterity.

Mentally, surgeons must be able to maintain their focus for long periods of time. Even a small mistake can be fatal. And because surgeons never know what they will find once they cut into a patient, surgeons must be good problem solvers who are able to make quick decisions, often with limited information. They must be able to think on their feet and persevere even when faced with unexpected complications. This takes technical knowledge, confidence, and the ability to remain calm under stressful circumstances.

Surgeons demand a lot from themselves and from the surgical team. Successful surgeons are often perfectionists. They should be comfortable being a team leader, have good communication skills in order to motivate and instruct the team, and be willing to take responsibility for all outcomes. Indeed, even with the best of care some patients do not survive, or surgery may not cure their problem. Surgeons should be emotionally strong and stable. In order to maintain their mental health and do their job well, they must be able to accept these situations without becoming emotionally involved.

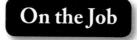

On the Job

Employers

Most surgeons are self-employed or are in partnership with other physicians; some are employed by hospitals, outpatient surgical centers, or the military.

Working Conditions

Most surgeons typically work four to five days per week, and they are usually on call for emergencies. Including time in surgery, office hours, administrative duties, and on-call time, it is not unusual for a surgeon to work between fifty and sixty hours per week. Caseloads vary. On average, a surgeon performs three hundred to four hundred surgeries annually.

Most surgeons maintain medical offices where they hold pre- and postsurgery consultations with patients. When performing surgery, surgeons work in a sterile environment. They are routinely exposed to blood, bodily fluids, and infectious disease. Wearing a surgical mask, gloves, and gown and washing hands before and after surgery helps lessen a surgeon's risk of contracting or spreading infection.

Earnings

The BLS reports the average mean salary for a surgeon is $231,550. However, a surgeon's earnings vary greatly, depending on the specialty field. For instance, a 2011 survey conducted by the American Medical Group Association, an organization that represents medical groups, reported the following median annual salary for the following surgical specialists: cardiac and thoracic, $544,087; colorectal, $405,000; general, $370,024; neurological, $656,250; orthopedic, $515,759; pediatric $463,801; and trauma, $414,993. The location of the practice also affects earnings. According to the BLS, the best-paying states for surgeons are Wyoming, Wisconsin, Washington, Tennessee, and South Dakota.

Since most surgeons are self-employed, they do not receive employee benefits such as health insurance, paid vacation and sick days, or retirement benefits. Surgeons who are employed by hospitals, other medical facilities, or the military, however, usually receive these benefits.

Opportunities for Advancement

Salaried surgeons can expect advancement based on their years of experience and job performance. Self-employed surgeons can increase their caseload, which yields increased income. Gaining certification also helps surgeons advance in the field. Certified surgeons can become part of a medical school faculty. They can also advance to an administrative position as the head of the surgical department of a hospital or other health care facility.

What Is the Future Outlook for Surgeons?

The BLS predicts that employment for surgeons will increase by 24 percent between 2010 and 2020. Top employment opportunities are predicted to be in rural and low-income areas that typically have trouble attracting physicians.

Find Out More

American Association for Academic Surgery
11300 W. Olympic Blvd., Suite 600
Los Angeles, CA 90064
phone: (310) 437-1606
website: www.aasurg.org

This association of surgeons offers visitors to its website an online streaming video documentary titled *Redefining Surgery*, which provides individuals interested in a career as a surgeon with lots of information about the profession.

American Board of Surgery (ABS)
1617 John F. Kennedy Blvd., Suite 860
Philadelphia, PA 19103
phone: (215) 568-4000
website: www.absurgery.org

The ABS conducts certifying exams and provides surgeons with specialty certification. In addition to information about certification and certifying exams, the website gives descriptions of various surgical specialties and offers related links to surgical specialty organizations and career information.

American College of Surgeons
633 N. Saint Clair St.
Chicago, IL 60611-3211
phone: (312) 202-5000
website: www.facs.org

The American College of Surgeons is a scientific and educational association of surgeons dedicated to providing surgical patients with quality care. Among other activities, it provides the public with information about surgeons and surgery. Visitors to the website can access information about a career as a surgeon.

Association of Women Surgeons
5204 Fairmount Ave.
Downers Grove, IL 60515
phone: (708) 226-2725
e-mail: info@womensurgeons.org
website: www.womensurgeons.org

This association supports women surgeons. Its *Pocket Mentor Handbook*, which is available on the website, provides information about the career, medical school, and the transition from medical school student to resident to practicing surgeon.

Interview with a Mental Health Counselor

Gilbert Morales is a mental health counselor at Esperanza Guidance Services Incorporated in Las Cruces, New Mexico. He has worked as a mental health counselor for fifteen years. He specializes in mental health and alcohol/drug abuse counseling. He answered questions about his career by e-mail and telephone.

Q: Why did you become a mental health counselor?
A: I have always liked to work with people. I wanted to help people learn to help themselves with their problems and provide them with the skills they need to avoid future problems.

Q: Can you describe a typical workday?
A: I work long hours, usually 9:00 a.m. to 7:00 p.m. Monday through Friday. I work until 7:00 p.m. so that clients who have to work during the day can make it to counseling sessions. We're here to accommodate their schedule.

I see individual clients and conduct group psychotherapy sessions. Each group session centers on a particular issue, specific to the group members like anger management, substance abuse, or PTSD (post-traumatic stress disorder). In group sessions, we work on how to identify triggers that lead to the particular problem and how to cope with these triggers in a more positive way. In individual sessions, I use different types of therapy techniques. What I use depends on the clients, their problems, and what works best for them.

Most of my clients attend one hour-long individual session per week and one hour-long group session per week for at least twelve weeks. Before they can begin attending sessions, I do an initial clinical assessment in which I interview the client to determine his or her problem and give a diagnosis. After that, I develop a treatment plan that includes how to treat the problem and the treatment goals.

Once a week, I also attend staffing meetings in which I meet with coworkers, social workers, and our clinical director to discuss our cases.

Q: What do you like most and least about your job?

A: The thing I like most is seeing people learn how to cope with their illness (both addictions and mental health), especially when initially I see people come in who are hurting, and when they leave they have a job, a home. They are no longer in jail or spending all their money on drugs. That is very rewarding. It's also rewarding to know that what I do helps families and society. For example, if a father is an addict, his addiction may cause him to be abusive to his wife and children. Helping him, helps make his wife and children safer and happier, and helps society overall.

The thing I like least is the paperwork. We must document each client's symptoms, diagnosis, and how each person progresses. We need documentation to get paid, for insurance purposes, and it is essential for medical and legal purposes. For me, it is the least desirable part of my job, but it is also very important because we must keep accurate records.

Q: What personal qualities do you find valuable for this type of work?

A: The most valuable qualities needed to do this type of work are genuinely caring about others. Patience and empathy are essential. So is being non-judgmental. You have to have a genuine desire to help and understand people without judging them. You also have to maintain professional ethics. Maintaining confidence of what you hear and see is essential to this job.

Q: What advice do you have for students who might be interested in this career?

A: If you like psychology, take as many courses as you can in this field. Also, talk to a mental health counselor and ask him or her to answer your questions about the field of psychology. Be prepared to go to college. You will need to get an advanced degree in the field of psychology and be licensed by the state where you practice.

Q: How did you train for your career?

A: I have a Master's degree in Counseling Psychology from New Mexico State University and a Doctorate degree in General Psychology from Capella University. Before becoming licensed and earning my degree, I had to do extensive field experience under the supervision of a licensed counselor, and I had to pass a licensing exam. To maintain my license, I have to take forty continuing education credits in my field each year. So, you're never through with your education. You have to always keep current with what is going on in mental health counseling.

Q: What is one thing you would like to tell young people about your career?

A: As time passes more and more individuals need your help, for example, veterans with PTSD, substance abuse dependent individuals and their families. The world is getting more and more complex each year and the challenges people face are enormous. You can make a difference in people's lives.

Other Jobs in Health Care

Acupuncturist
Anesthesiologist
Art therapist
Athletic trainer
Audiologist
Biomedical engineer
Biomedical equipment
   technician
Chiropractor
Dental assistant
Dental hygienist
Dental laboratory technician
Dentist
Dietitian
Epidemiologist
Forensic pathologist
Genetic counselor
Health care manager
Health educator
Health information
   management technician
Massage therapist

Medical secretary
Medical social worker
Medical technologist
Music therapist
Nurse's aide
Occupational therapist
Optician
Optometrist
Orthotists/Prosthetists
Paramedic
Perfusionist
Pharmacist
Pharmacy technician
Phlebotomist
Physical therapy assistant
Physician
Physician's assistant
Podiatrist
Psychiatrist
Rehabilitation counselor
Speech-language pathologist
Surgical technologist

Editor's Note: The online *Occupational Outlook Handbook* of the US Department of Labor's Bureau of Labor Statistics is an excellent source of information on jobs in hundreds of career fields including many of those listed here. The *Occupational Outlook Handbook* may be accessed online at www.bls.gov/ooh/.

Index

About the Author

Barbara Sheen is the author of more than eighty books for young people. She lives in New Mexico with her family. In her spare time she likes to swim, cook, walk, garden, and read.